M000306398

KINGDOM BUILDERS

IN BUSINESS

HOW PAIN, PASSION, PURPOSE INSPIRED A FAITH JOURNEY TO ENTREPRENEURSHIP

COMPILED BY JOAN T RANDALL

FOREWARD BY CHETWYN PETE CAMPUS PASTOR ELEVATION UC

KINGDOM BUILDERS IN BUSINESS

Published by Victorious You

Copyright @ 2020 Joan T Randall

Printed in the Unites States of America

First Printing, 2020

ISBN: 978-1-7340609-1-1

For details email Joan T Randall

joan@joantrandall.com or call 980-785-4959

www.joantrandall.com

DEDICATION

This book is dedicated

To the men and women who are business leaders;

and have the gift of generosity and commitment

to expanding the Kingdom of God

through purpose, people, and partnerships.

Table of Contents

FOREWARD

As a pastor, I am always trying to figure out how to bring people together in a world that can be so divisive. One of the ways we do this at our church is to connect people in the same season of life or with similar interests. I started to think of my life's journey and realized how much business and entrepreneurship meant to me. My dad had multiple businesses, one of which was our family corner store. He gave me a chance to work there to make some money to finance my love for the mall. My brother became a barber in the back of the store as well.

As I thought about that season of life, I couldn't help but think of the fun, laughter, and joy that came from running our own business. On the other hand, I remember some of the obstacles and heartache my family walked through during those years as well. This led to me having an idea to bring business leaders and entrepreneurs together. We wanted to create space for leaders to learn from each other, provide resources, and a community that focused on faith. I wondered what would have happened if my family had a community like this.

I had no idea God would use this prompting of mine to produce a renewed passion and purpose in the authors of

"Kingdom Builders in Business." This is more than a book about business and entrepreneurship. You will be inspired by the faith and perseverance of these men and women as you read their stories. We are all different, but it's something about pain, struggles, and faith that will always unify us. I believe you will find yourself in their vulnerability, and my prayer is that this book would give you the courage to not give up. I hope that you would be inspired to use your gifts and talents to walk in your God-given purpose.

Pastor Chetwyn Pete Campus Pastor,

Elevation Church University City, Charlotte NC

INTRODUCTION

When I got the phone call asking me if I would consider taking on the leader's role for the Entrepreneur eGroup at Elevation University City, I was surprised. My first thoughts were me? Then something dropped in my spirit and said, why not you? I was unaware that there was such a group, but then again, I had only joined the church five months earlier. I told the caller that I was currently leading an eGroup, and I loved my group. His next statement led me to believe that he had made his decision and that I was the person he wanted. He shared with me that he had been watching my social media pages for a while and that it was clear to him that I possessed the professional and personal skillsets that would make me a great leader for the Entrepreneur group. His words humbled me. Then he asked, "Is there someone in your current group that would be able to step up and lead?" I told him that there was a possibility. He mentioned that the current leader of the group was relocating, and he wanted to have someone in place so she could turn things over. As he was sharing with me about the history of the group, I started to feel excited about the possibilities. When he asked me if I had any thoughts on how I wanted to lead the group, I gave him a litany of ideas. They

3

rolled off my tongue without me having to think too deep. I assumed the role two months later.

My first official Entrepreneur eGroup meeting was May 2019; only six people showed up, despite a roster that showed 48 members. We made the most of it and had a great time. One of the items on the agenda was an Anthology. I told the group that we would be writing a book together as an end of year project. I think that stunned the group. Here I was, a new leader, and at my very first meeting, I am sharing with the group that we will be writing a book together. I understood the questionable looks from the group, but it fueled me to show them what God could do through us. I assured them that if they were interested, we could work together and make it happen, and it would give them momentum for their business.

My co-leader Tami and I kept showing up for meetings despite the low participation, and soon we started averaging fifteen to twenty-five eGroup members when we meet. Our goal was to provide them with all the tools they needed to be successful in their businesses. We invited subject matter experts as special guest speakers to come in and share their business expertise with the group. It gave them significant value.

In September 2019, I held our first Anthology interest meeting, and twenty-five people said yes to writing a book. When all was said and done, only twelve people committed to moving forward. I thought long and hard about whether or not I should continue. It would have been easy for me to say let's cancel it all together because of the lack of interest, but the follow up meeting two weeks later changed every thought I had about canceling.

This meeting, in particular, was where I gave all the information and answered every question about Anthologies. There was a lot of dialogue among the group members. I decided to go around the room and ask each individual why they wanted to be a part of this book. The answers were a little surprising. In my mind, I thought Entrepreneurs were risk-takers, but I soon found out that was not the case when it came to writing a book. As each person spoke, the Holy Spirit kept saying, "See what God can do through you." Everyone in that room wanted to write a book or had the desire to write a book, but so many things prevented them from doing so. I heard words like fear, doubt, not good enough, embarrassed to share my story, not knowing how or where to start, the process seemed daunting. As each of them shared a piece of their story, I knew that we were on to something. One story, however, tugged at my heart and almost brought me to tears. This individual was a senior, and she had dreams of publishing short stories. She owns a journal filled with several short stories but never got an opportunity to publish any and thought she would never be able to do so. Her exact words were, "I thought I would leave this earth without getting a chance to become an author; thank you for making this possible for me." Immediately tears

welled up in my eyes, and I felt a presence in the room. I knew it was the Holy Spirit telling me to move forward. God showed me that this was my chance to see what He would do through the willing members who said Yes and me. I recognized that the number twelve was significant, and I was convinced and convicted that it was God's plan. I knew I had to move forward. I did it for her, I did it for them, I did it to honor my Senior Pastor who leads by example, I did it to praise God, and the community that he allowed me to lead.

What a great accomplishment. If God gives you the vision, He will provide you with the resources to bring it to fruition. All it takes is a little mustard seed faith with intentional action. This process has been a faith walk for each of the Co-Author. They will forever be known as Kingdom Builders Published Authors. They will never forget the day they joined the Entrepreneur eGroup at Elevation Church University City, where they experienced care and community and dared to allow God to use them. This process reminds me of the scripture; *I can do all things through Christ - Philippians 4:13.*

As one of our Co-Authors so eloquently put it: "I will persevere to see what God will do through me as His kingdom builder. He has empowered me to remember him, for it is he that giveth thee **power to get wealth,** that he may establish his covenant which he swore unto thy fathers, as it is this day. "– Moreale Brown

ACKNOWLEDGMENTS

I feel blessed to see this book come to life. I am incredibly grateful to the twelve authors who said yes! They were willing to go on this faith journey with me to see what God could do through us:

Tami S, Venita J, Moreale B, Reneè C, Kine T, Gen C, Ebonee L, Rene B, Tamra , Belinda S, Stephanie M, and Juanita J, you have shared a piece of you with the world. I know that through your stories, lives will be changed. You are all so amazing, and I am grateful to you.

Venita J, co-author, and cover designer. Thank you for not only sharing your story but for lending your gifts and talent into creating the amazing graphics for the book cover. You are gifted; thank you for being able to see the vision of what we wanted to portray.

Moreale B, co-author, and marketing lead. Thank you for partnering with me to do the marketing and promotions for the book; you are truly incredible.

Tami S, co-author and co-leader of the Entrepreneur group. You have been my partner in this group from the beginning. Thank you for leading with honesty and integrity and for allowing me to have a safe space to bounce ideas. You are a quiet storm, an introvert who becomes extroverted when it is necessary. You are my champion.

Rosalyn Robinson, my friend and prayer warrior. You made this all possible, and I will always honor you as the sower who planted a seed that leads to the birthing of several harvests. If you had not reached out to me and invited me to Elevation church, this book would not have been born. Your daily inspirational quotes and prayer calls to me drew me into a space that changed my life, and my spiritual walk with God. Thank you for being obedient to the Holy Spirit, thank you for always showing up, thank you for your support and thank you for leading me to the place I now call home. Kingdom Builders in Business is your book as well, and I hope you are proud of it. I will always cherish our friendship.

Matt McAndrew, Elevation UC eGroup Director. Thank you for meeting with me and sharing in the excitement as I told you about our project. You were just as enthusiastic as I was. You saw that this book was more significant than just our eGroup, and you partnered with Pastor Chet to see how we could use this model as an example of a community for other eGroups. Thank you for believing in us.

Pastor Chetwyn Pete, I honor you as the leader of our campus. You started the group, and we wanted to carry on with your vision of care, collaboration, and community within the group. You took this process a step further and got Elevation

Central involved to see how we could use this book at our campus. Thank you for trusting us to deliver not only the stories but a workbook than can be incorporated into Elevation UC's curriculum. You did that, and it empowered the co-authors way beyond their imagination. You are a true visionary.

Angela M Haigler, my Limitless Lifestyle partner, and Senior Editor. Thank you for the editorial insights and changes that were necessary for the book to flow. You are more than just the editor; you took on each story as if it was your own and brought life to them. Thank you for going on this journey with me.

Tony Rushing of 180° Productions, videographer/ photographer. You dropped everything and said yes to accommodating the co-authors who needed to get their headshots. You went above and beyond to get the photos back to me within a day or two of taking them. Thank you for your friendship and partnership. I appreciate you and Nikki.

Katie Ohlin, you gave me the first opportunity to lead an eGroup at Elevation church. I remembered our first interview at Starbucks. Your calm and kind spirit allowed me to share my whole life story with you. I will never forget.

Colin Cruz, I am indebted to you. You saw something in me and saw it fit to ask me to be the leader of the group. We are here because of you.

Matthew Hines, Lani van Heerden, Anyel Albury, you all believed in me and allowed me to be my authentic self. Because of that, I took to heart the words, "To see what God can do through me." You guys have poured into me, prayed for me, and encouraged me since I got to Elevation Church. Thank you.

Kay and Shay, my beautiful girls. I am who I am because of you. You both represent the best of who I am, and the best of who God created me to be. My favorite job is being your Mother. Thank you for your love and support. My legacy belongs to you and my grandbabies.

Brianna and Brandon, my love children. My life is enhanced because of your presence. I love you both so much. Thank you for allowing me to share some space with your mom.

Bill Randall, my husband, and my everything on this side of heaven. There are no words in any language that can express my love, appreciation, gratitude, and respect for you. In you, I found my Boaz. You built a foundation of love, support, kindness, and equality in our home on which I stand. I climb, I grow, I elevate, I soar because you give me wings. I love you beyond love.

O IS FOR OBEDIENCE

Tami L Stewart

"You're wasting your time with that silly stuff, no one cares about your hobby."

"No one is going to want that; you can't make money with that."

"You will never be on my level, that's just a hobby. What I do makes money."

"Other women do... Other women wear..."

"You have an inability to communicate. You're that way because of your family."

"You'll never find another man like me."

"If you don't like it, you can ease on down the road."

These are statements I often heard from my narcissistic spouse of nine years. I refuse to use the terms husband or marriage because I never had either of those things during my time with him. By definition, narcissists often have an inflated view of themselves. They tend to belittle the abilities, gifts, and talents of those in close relationships with them. They are arrogant, lack empathy, and feel genuinely entitled. Narcissists are generally hypersensitive due to their extreme insecurities, so communication with them is challenging. My spouse always

11

criticized me: What I did, how I looked, what I thought, and how I spoke. I realize now he acted to make himself feel superior and further reinforce his belief that I was inferior.

Over time this type of verbal and emotional abuse began to destroy my self-confidence. He was relentless in the war he waged against me. Between his constant criticisms, his frequent ranting about how awful my friends were, and the daily berating of my family, I began to doubt my own reality. I could never win an argument because he was always right, and anything I said was irrelevant or insignificant. I finally released my need to win disagreements with my spouse when my dad said, "Stop all the back and forth! You cannot reason with an irrational person, it's a waste of your energy." He was right. I saved my energy, but I ended up feeling like a shell of a person, just going along with whatever, he said in hopes of holding onto a little peace of mind.

When I think back to the beginning of our relationship, I see now the narcissistic tendencies were always there. But I was young and in love, blinded by his smile and good looks. I thought the feeling was mutual, but there always seemed to be another woman in the picture. There was never any proof at first, but once I found out narcissists needed a harem of women to shore up their bad feelings about themselves, things that did not seem quite right before we got married, began to make more sense. The irony of my story is the fact that the Lord gave me so many opportunities to escape the torment that lay ahead of me, but I didn't see them at the time. Then when I did recognize the Lord's voice in later years, I was still disobedient to His word. I felt compelled to read and listen to the word, but I didn't really understand how to apply it to my everyday life. A positive outcome of my situation was unveiling. The beginning of my relationship with the narcissist was also the beginning of my faith walk.

By nature, I have always tried to do the right thing. I treat others the way I want to be treated and have turned the other cheek more times than I can count. I tend to take commitment seriously, especially when it comes to relationships. In the beginning, I placed more attention on my relationship with the narcissist than on walking in faithful obedience, trusting, and believing in the Lord's will for my life. As my faith began to grow, I started to put more focus on the Lord and less on the narcissist.

Nonetheless, the narcissist was still focused on trying to make every aspect of my life miserable. We dated for three years, had a bad break up, and then got back together two years later. That break up was one of the first opportunities that God placed before me to be free, but I didn't listen. I didn't know that narcissists will say or do anything to reel their victim back into the relationship. He used religion like a carrot dangled in front of an unsuspecting rabbit. He was a "changed man," he said. I believed him and allowed him to re-enter my life.

At that time in my faith walk, I was living a celibate life. I told him premarital sex was not an option. Within no time, marriage was put on the table, and I reluctantly said yes. However, since I had prayed about it, and things appeared to be moving in the right direction, I thought being married to him was the Lord's will. What I later realized is that I really prayed for my will, not the Lord's will, and God gave me what I asked for. That reluctance I felt was likely another message from God. Once again, I didn't listen.

On our first wedding anniversary, my gift to him was a box with a book of baby names, a little plastic stork, and a copy of an ultrasound. We were having a baby! Since he insisted that I stop using birth control immediately after our wedding day, I thought he would be thrilled about becoming a father. I envisioned a happy, peaceful pregnancy. No such luck! My first trimester was horrible. Most reasonable people understand the fact that you have absolutely no energy and sleep a lot during that time. It was even in our "What to Expect While Expecting" book. Seeing it in black and white was still not good enough for him. He accused me of being lazy and woke me up any time he saw me asleep. Even after I worked all day and made dinner that evening, I still could not have a peaceful nap.

Once the baby was born, he was of little or no help. The majority of the responsibility for raising our child fell on me. Yes, narcissists do not take or accept responsibility and usually blame others for things that don't go as they have planned. The narcissist was fired from his job six months after our son was born. An opportunity arose for him to work out of town, which he gladly accepted. You see, this freed him up from the responsibility of being a spouse and father. It also created the perfect environment for numerous infidelities. He was working out of town during the week and would arrive at home on Saturday mornings. Oddly enough, every Saturday, he needed to go to either the electronic or music store and then was gone the remainder of the day. As a result, very little time was spent with his son or me. Looking back on it, he was more than likely cheating with someone from his harem.

After nearly two years of him working out of town during the week, I got laid off from my job. At this point, it made sense for us just to move to be closer to the location of his job so the "family" could be together. A month or so before me relocating, a mutual friend called to tell me the Lord spoke to her in a dream and told her to give me the message. She said she would rather tell me face-to-face and asked if I would come to her house. When I arrived, she seemed a little uneasy and hesitant, but went on to say the Lord told her my spouse was trying to kill me. She grabbed my hand and said, not in the physical sense but in the spiritual sense. She then went on to say, you should not relocate to an area where you have no support network because he is trying to isolate you from friends and family. Looking back, I recognize this was another chance to escape and the first act of disobedience.

I did end up moving away from everyone and everything familiar to me for a little over two years. During this period, I felt as if the narcissist was strategically trying to chip away at anything positive about me or surrounding me. This was also when I started to disconnect from our so-called marriage mentally. We sought marital counseling, not by my choice, but his suggestion. In our very first session, the counselor apparently recognized his narcissism. She told him she believed he wanted to go to counseling just to have someone confirm everything he said or thought about me. She went on to say if he had a list of things for me to do and I did everything on it, she believed he would still find something to complain about.

When I had my one-on-one session, she said, "I am out of line by saying this, but why are you still with him? It is clear that he has no regard for you." I told her that I am here for my child. Once the therapist told the narcissist that I was not going to think like him, act like him or talk like him because I am an individual; he got uneasy. Once she said I had my own mind and was capable of having my opinion about doing or saying things the way I choose, counseling was over. It was back to the regular attack. Shortly after that, we moved back home. Still committed to my vows as a wife, I agreed to look for a new home to purchase for the "family." We decided on new construction and found what we thought would be the perfect home.

Fast forward to January 2006, our newly constructed home was complete. Our closing date was set for February 17, 2006. Two weeks before the closing, during a walk-through of the home, I heard the Lord clearly say, "Do not close on this house." I questioned what I heard, asking, "What Lord?" Again I heard, "DO NOT CLOSE ON THIS HOUSE!" Feeling conflicted, confused, and not knowing what to do since my mind told me that perhaps this house and this stability would be suitable for the family. My son was now five years old, and we had already moved six times. Once he saw the house, he asked, "Mommy, when we move in here, will we have to move again?" I told him no, we will not have to move again; this will be our home for a long time, which led him to jump for joy. My mind was still focused on stability and one last-ditch effort to keep the "family" together. So again, I was disobedient to Lord, and that resulted in what I thought was going to be a fairytale ending turning into a year of living hell.

From the moment we signed on the dotted line, there was a new level of narcissism to experience right down to the simplest of things. For example, if I turned on the porch light, he would turn it off. If I put the trash can on one side of the house, he would come home and immediately put it on the other side. It was so bad that if I said the sky was blue, he would say it was black just to disagree with me. It seemed like his goal was to aggravate and provoke me in any way he could, like following me from room to room, arguing over the pettiest of things. I soon discovered he had taken my phones to delete mean text messages he had sent me and then forwarded what was considered damaging to his phone from mine. Things got to the point where I had to sleep with my phone and car keys in my pillowcase or my underwear because his actions were so unpredictable. One night in particular, after trying to escape the madness, I broke down crying uncontrollably. I screamed out to the Lord, "Why are you allowing these things to happen to me? Haven't I tried to live right? To provide stability for my son, my family?"

God's reply was swift. He told me He was making me strong, so I could be a testimony for other women. Clearly, He knew more about what I could bear than I did. Soon after that message from the Lord, I realized I had endured enough of the narcissistic abuse. I had put up with far more than anyone should ever have to. So, with a clear conscience and with the Lord to guide me, I chose to exit the crazy, roller coaster ride of marriage. Just like Dorothy from the Wiz, I found the courage to "ease-on-down, ease-on-down-the-road," as the narcissist had been suggesting I do for years. I was emotionally ready. Six months later, while at the beach for a weekend of meditation, I clearly heard the Lord say, "It is time." This time I was obedient to his voice. When I returned home, things fell into place for me to move on February 17, 2007, one year to the date of the closing on that house.

Throughout that year of hell, I was prompted to go back to doing some of the things that had previously given me joy in my life. I loved crafts and making jewelry, but the chaotic environment caused by the narcissist was never conducive to my creativity. At that time, I did not know that making jewelry and other crafts could become my supplemental income and lead me down the path to entrepreneurship. The narcissist certainly never encouraged my burgeoning talent. Going through the divorce process was not easy as I spent nine months going back and forth to court to resolve custody and child support issues. After leaving the courthouse for the eighth time, I walked across the street with tears streaming down my face, wondering why I had to keep going through that drama. Suddenly I heard the Lord say, "I want you to trust and believe solely in me."

Thinking I was trusting in Him, I started joining different multi-level marketing companies trying to make up for the lack of child support. What I really did was grasp at straws in desperation, and ultimately those opportunities did not work. Once again, He told me to trust and believe in Him. God reminded me of the gifts and talents that He had given me and told me to stop following others and use those gifts. Once I raised my hands in complete obedience, submitting my will and asking for the Lord's will to be done in my life, everything started to fall in place. I am grateful for the paths the Lord has allowed me to follow and cross on this journey. If it were not for all of my experiences along the way, I would not be the strong woman I am today. God's word came to pass just as He said. At my most painful point, the Lord answered my cries and assured my experience was not in vain. I was broken down to become durable and to help others through my testimony. My company, Totally Tamz, was born. I design beautiful and affordable jewelry, and that income has allowed me to support a son who is now in college financially.

And God willing, I may now have an opportunity to teach crafts to women who have re-entered society after incarceration. The goal is to provide an income-producing skill for them to learn and, if interested, help them on the path toward entrepreneurship.

REBORN

Renée Cholmondeley

From the Urban Dictionary:

1. Renée

A French name meaning "rebirth" or "renaissance."

People with this name tend to be idealistic, highly imaginative, intuitive, and spiritual. They seek after spiritual truth and often find it. They tend to be visionary thinkers and may inspire others.

Renée is amazing. She's random, weird, and somewhat insecure. In addition to being outspoken, she is fiercely loyal to her friends. Renée is beautiful inside and out, open-minded, mean at times, dedicated to music, and impulsive. She can be a hypocrite but owns up to it rather than denying it. She may not always use her head; most times, she uses her heart. She tends to make excuses for the people she cares about. People with this name have a deep inner desire for a stable, loving family or community, a need to work with others, and to be appreciated.

Renée is the female form of René, which is the French form of the late Roman name Renatus. The meaning is reborn or born again. In medieval times, the meaning was associated with the Christian concept of being spiritually born again through baptism. The definition 'reborn' implies not an actual rebirth but a spiritual or intellectual rebirth, a reawakening.

I wonder if my mother knew the meaning of my name when she *blessed* me with it. Was it intentional? I doubt it because She was only 13 or 14 years old when she gave birth to me. And I can't ask Her because She is not present in my life. Alive and well but still not present in my life. Maybe She just liked the name? It is a lovely name, and I love it! I don't ever recall Her being loving or affectionate to me, which makes me believe naming me couldn't have come from a loving place.

Born again and again….

I'm sure she didn't know that she was being prophetic by naming me Renée. Because for me to maintain my sanity and not check out, I've needed to have multiple rebirths. I lived in the shadow and the shame of Her rejection for most of my life. The whispers behind my back. *What kind of person is she whose own mother does not love her? What God-awful thing did she do to cause her mother to cast her out?* Many times, being told that I "must have done something wrong" because mothers don't just simply refuse to love their children. The rumors still fly! I've lived most of my life thinking that if my own mother did not love me, why should anyone else? Then I spent a good chunk of it trying to prove to everyone around me that I was worthy of being loved.

But God...

My life is a series of rebirths. I have been renewed, transformed, and reborn many times. Sometimes the renewal feels as if from moment to moment, and other times the feeling is more season to season. I can recall times in my life that I look back, and I'm amazed at what I've survived: childhood sexual abuse, emotional, psychological, and physical abuse and homelessness. In my late teens and early twenties, people who knew my story, would boldly and somewhat disrespectfully tell me that they were surprised that I didn't end up on the streets, a drug-addicted hooker. I was a good kid for the most part. I can say that with pure confidence at this stage in my life, having raised my own kids to adulthood. Like most adolescents, I was far from perfect, but I did well in school, made the honor roll most of the time, and did my chores. I had a part-time job before I was old enough to work legally. There wasn't a time when I didn't have dreams and aspirations. I often thought about how my life would be as an adult and how I would be the change that the world needs.

But God!

For so long, I didn't know that my life and my existence on this planet really mattered to anyone, but God and I didn't meet Him until I was 21 years old. Since then, I've just been trying to live out the Love that He has already demonstrated to me. As a little girl and well into adulthood, I always thought that there was something wrong with me. I was always different from the rest of the kids in my extended family and at school. Even though I felt "less-than," deep down inside, I always felt strongly that I was here to do something special. Still, I never shared my secret purpose with anyone else.

I was left by the young girl who gave birth to me and raised by my grandmother in South Carolina. There I lived with my grandmother and her youngest and oldest son, my uncles. My mother left the south as many Black people did in the sixties and migrated to the north in search of a "better" life. She moved to New York City when I was just 3 years old and returned to South Carolina 2-3 times a year. She always floated into town in style, looking and smelling pretty and smoking long slim cigarettes. She was a beautiful woman. Hair was done up, make-up flawless, and wearing the latest fashions on her long-legged, thoroughbred figure. She was fun-loving and full of laughter. The party started as soon as she arrived. Records stacked up on the stereo in the order they would be played, drinks poured. The driveway filled up with the cars of family and friends who couldn't wait to lay eyes on her! It seemed like the whole town was excited about her coming home. Strangers would come up to me in the weeks before her arrival and say, "You must be so glad that 'yo mama is coming home soon!"

But I never was. It took me until the age of 50 before I realized the anxiety that I felt on those visits. It was never a fun time for me. For the week or two, while she was there, my whole life turned upside down. It was fine while all the partying was going on. I got to see my cousins for extended periods. The adults were in such a celebratory mood, and so they were very lenient. We got to go to the store whenever we wanted, played outside after dark, and we would sneak and smoke cigarettes at the back of the house. We didn't have to go to church on Sunday morning - She didn't go to church. She always came home with a suitcase full of new clothes and shoes for me and sometimes for my grandmother too. I remember how the new clothes smell filled up the bedroom. Everyone wanted to see what she brought me, oohing and ahhing at everything, telling me how lucky I was. Some of my female cousins would get jealous and say things like, "you think you something cause 'yo momma live in New Yawk."

Monday morning, after all the partying, I got to try on all my new clothes. She would take Polaroid pictures of me in my outfits, maybe to show her boyfriends and friends back in New York. I had to take them off afterward because these clothes were for school and church. Then I got to run errands with her, always a few steps behind, as she switched up and down the street, stopping traffic. Men would hang their heads out of windows as they passed to get a better look at her and say things that I was way too young to understand. Yeah, life in the town would get turned upside down for a week or two while She was there. I dreaded Her visits because I knew I was going to catch hell. It was inevitable that I would get my behind beat, "so I wouldn't be able to sit down!" at some point during her "vacation." Sometimes it was an open display. She'd go to the front yard or out to the field beside the house to pick a switch off the tree. We would watch her sit on the front porch and "clean" it - pulling all the leaves off it, so the little bumps where the stalks used to be were sure to teach me a lesson. Sometimes it was a belt, and other times her open palm was enough if it needed to be quick. There was always a list of things that I was doing wrong. I just never knew how she came up with it. I could have been prepared if I knew how she got the list. I remember more than once getting beat for "lying" for just being a horrible liar, but I had no idea what I had lied about.

I don't ever remember any loving and affectionate times between us. I don't ever remember feeling that I was special to her. I could feel her look at me as if I was a reminder of things simply gone wrong. I always felt like I interrupted her life. I'm sure I was an embarrassment to her; I get the sense that she had big dreams too. There was always something wrong with me: my hair was broken and dry, I was too skinny, my knees were scarred up, I was too ashy, my teeth were crooked, I smelled bad. The list went on and on. I don't ever remember her hugging me when she arrived in town or when she left for that matter. She hugged my grandmother, uncles, aunts, and cousins. I always wondered why she didn't hug me. I remember her scolding me, telling me to make sure I helped my grandmother keep the house clean and to do well in school as she walked out the door. I'm not trying to paint a picture of a monster - as I genuinely don't believe she is a horrible person. I think that she did the best she could with what she had. I even think she may have loved me at some point. I believe that when people know better, they do better.

I believe she was then and is now just a scared, hurt individual. I yearn to know what happened to her to cause her to make the choices she does. Things did go wrong obviously as she was just a child, barely a teenager when she became pregnant with me. The lack of love and rejection I felt from her caused me to allow similar treatment from others. I embraced that wrongly downloaded data for far too long in my life. I lived most of my life feeling like I was just all wrong.

But God…

When my grandmother became ill, I had just entered puberty. She decided that it was too much of a burden for my grandmother to continue to take care of me, so she took me to New York City to live with her and her husband. Soon after, she "accidentally" fostered my interest in fashion, garment construction, styling. While unintentional, she helped bring out the innate, raw talent that my Creator gifted me with. These projects would keep me busy for hours at a time and became my "babysitter" since I was just 13 years old but too old for a traditional sitter. Then she and my stepfather could go on movie dates. One project came on an insert in the T.V. Guide. It gave instructions on how to convert a pair of denim jeans into a skirt by deconstructing the jeans and reconstructing the pieces to form a denim skirt magically. It was everything! I was smitten! Shortly before, she had already taught me how to use a sewing machine. Later, her method would be the exact same one my design teacher used to instruct my class on how to sew in my freshman year at the High School of Fashion Industries.

Look at God!

I was always afraid of her and held reverent respect for her as most everyone who knew her did. I would never dispute anything she ever said. The only time I ever challenged her was when I was accepted into the school that was dedicated to fashion. She refused to allow me to attend. This was so confusing to me because she had taught me to use a sewing machine and how to cut patterns. She allowed me to apply to the school, create a portfolio, take the exam, and go for the entrance interview. Many were turned away, but I was accepted right away, yet she forbid me to go! She insisted that I attend a school for computer programming. I'm a creative, not an analytical person. While she was very insightful, she never saw me… she refused to, and she couldn't see me.

I excelled at the High School of Fashion Industries, stood out in my class even while my home life was very tumultuous.

My stepfather was physically abusive, and they were emotionally and psychologically abusive to one another. More often than not, our home was silent as they retreated to their respected corners in the house until they could get past their anger with one another. However, I managed to graduate with honors and was accepted into the coveted and prestigious Fashion Institute of Technology, where I excelled in my Fashion Design and Merchandising classes.

Unfortunately, it was a bit challenging as I found myself homeless just a month before the start of my first semester. On a typical Sunday afternoon, a few weeks after my stepfather had finally been removed from the home for battering her again, she complained about how bad I was at completing my chores. Like any typical parent-teen exchange, she heard me mumble under my breath that "I couldn't wait to grow up, move out and live on my own. That day she insisted that I do just that. Once that break was made, I didn't see or speak to Her again for over 12 years. Reborn...again. Being homeless with no physical address, I was unable to begin my studies at the start of the school year. I was, however, blessed to start in the spring semester-whew that was scary!

Thank you, God,...

Soon after leaving FIT, I quickly secured a role in a "hot" (that's how over-performing companies were referred to in the industry) junior sportswear company. I advanced very quickly to the position of East Coast Sales and Marketing Manager at just 20 years old. I later held titles as Product Development Specialist and V.P. of Design. I then went on to own and operate two more businesses in the fashion industry. My work has allowed me to travel to many cities in the U.S., Europe, and Asia. I've been blessed with a few awards in recognition for my work in my beloved rag trade.

As I lift my head in the stage of my life where wisdom has kicked in, I've learned that the Creator equips us with gifts wrapped in purpose so that we may fully complete our assignments here on Earth. Sometime in early 2010, that revelation came to me as I was sitting in a Sunday evening church service where one of the guest ministers was gospel great Marvin Winans. He spoke about what happens when your passion collides with your destiny, and at that moment, I discovered my purpose. The message referenced the entire 54th chapter of Isaiah, and this passage of scripture stirs my soul to this day. Verses 1-5 sang to me: Sing barren woman, you who never bore a child…I had had a couple of failed businesses that I called my "babies," and these verses resonated with me.

I realized then that every one of my life experiences had brought me to that moment. I felt so full afterward that I promptly began the planning of my next business. At that moment, I felt as if my passion collided with my purpose. I had a strong desire to create a destination business that would inspire confidence, support, and uplift women. I had always felt inspired to design and develop beautiful products for women. I had fulfilled multiple product development projects for many retailers, like Macy's, Sears & Ashley Stewart stores, but this was to be different. I felt the desire to interact directly with my clients, instead of just referencing them on the Monday morning sales reports. I wanted to be a "fashion consultant" to underserved women in my community. I'm Renée, owner/operator of Amused Designs, Inc.

Amused? A Muse is a divinely inspired creative being... Amused? Because I am finally and genuinely amused at life...

PAIN TO PURPOSE

Ebonee Bryant-Lindsay

Press on. Move Forward. Don't Stop. Never Give Up. Many of us have heard these phrases drilled into our heads since childhood. The encouraging words are a constant reminder that we must perform to the best of our abilities. Despite any struggles, we must push through.

I started my first job at sixteen, and, like most teenagers, I thought I had the world figured out. It's funny how my young mind was filled with the grandeur of what I thought life would be like for me. I figured if I just worked myself to the bone, I could obtain all that I dreamed of. So that's exactly what I did. I worked hard and tried to please everyone around me. If I could reach perfection, everything would work out as it should. Everyone would see my worthiness. Although I had a plan in mind of how I could reach my goals, I still wasn't exactly sure how to execute my plan. Let me introduce you to Lady Insecurity. She sways slowly and lingers, whispering in my ear, "You're too young to know what you want in life." "Nobody wants to hear what you have to say." "You're not that important." Lady Insecurity had me withering into a deep hole within myself. She made me feel like there was nothing special about me and that I had nothing to offer the world. Even though she whispered in my ear often, I pressed on.

I attended my first year of college at Eastern Michigan University in 2001 as an undeclared freshman. With prerequisites in hand and Lady Insecurity in my pocket, I began the search for my purpose in the world. I had dreams of becoming a woman of the Fine Arts, perhaps a songwriter, singer, or poet. Initially, I did not want to attend a university. Still, the pressure to be one of the first in our family to graduate from college influenced me to at least apply. I was taught that my success depended upon me walking the popular path of higher education. I walked, and then tripped the first year. I pushed on to the second year and even a third year until financial aid decided that I was not in the right place. I didn't know that college tuition would increase each year as the university saw fit. College financing 101 wasn't offered or explained. I wasn't aware that they could decide to cut my cash flow and say, "Nope, no more money for you, my dear."

Lady Insecurity sashayed into the corners of my mind. She spoke so sweetly, "See, I told you. They don't want you here. You're not talented enough for university, darling. University is for the people with the aptitude to make big things happen! You cannot afford the access to this higher level of knowledge. You're too poor, honey. You don't have it in you." Despite her whispers, I got a decent job and was determined to take care of myself and pursue my dreams anyway.

33

Did I tell you that love had made an entrance? Love had sauntered upon me and gave me the confidence that I could do anything. His name was Jonathan and we met our freshman year of college at Eastern Michigan University. We started dating at eighteen years old and moved in together in our twenties. Love flew in and with college slowly fading to the background due to finances, we began to find our footing in the world of adulthood. We moved to his hometown of Philadelphia and we began to map out our future. We both knew we wanted to become entrepreneurs. Jon would start his own martial arts school and I would be a writer. Life was good, but I still felt that I wasn't reaching my full potential. I was working a dead-end job that wasn't challenging and didn't utilize my skills. I tried to step back into the gleaming light of college life, but shortly fell into the black hole of financial struggles. Everyday living expenses took precedent over my higher education, as financial aid wasn't enough to cover the cost.

I decided I could never afford or have the wits to finish college. So reluctantly, I descended the stairs of excessively expensive academia and began to climb the standard and more popular corporate ladder. I gave myself endlessly to companies that had a hard time giving back. I thought, "Well, I guess this is how it's supposed to be. I kept giving my time, efforts, like, and love to a lot of people that didn't have space for it. So here she comes, Lady Insecurity. Getting louder, "Did you not hear me the first time?! You are not enough for these people in your life, honey. When will you get it through your head? People have better things to do than to be bothered with you!"

A vicious cycle, but I shut Lady Insecurity down, "Don't stop Ebonee. You can do this. You can be everything for everyone. You can be the best as long as you never give up." The confidence rises in my heart again despite the humming of internal defeat. I don't stop.

So, I continued to dive headfirst into adulthood, coming up for air only to explore splashing into the pool of parenthood. I could not wait to give my little one my unconditional love and support. Support can be a loving word and a weighty one. By definition, support means to bear all or part of the weight of; to hold up. In all the excitement of becoming a mother, I realized I didn't want just to support my future children. I wanted our lives to thrive. I didn't want my children to go through the same struggles. I didn't want to worry about how they would pay for college or how they could get a good job. He was just a little bean in my belly, and I was trying to figure out the world for him. I wanted to give him the best. We needed to provide him with financial freedom. As history shows us, freedom is a valuable commodity, fought, and sought after. Freedom often comes with a price, and I was willing to pay to ensure the success of our future generations. I worked full-time while learning how to build a business. I created a music blog featuring upcoming local artists. I thought if I created a forum for musicians, I could help propel their careers and my own.

I failed. It wasn't due to a lack of effort. Lady Insecurity was always at work. She never took a day off. She would continuously clock in with her barrage of commentary on the state of my life. "No one wants to read your blog. You don't even get any likes when you post online. No one is following you. Don't you have a child to raise? You should be concentrating on being a mother. How can you have time for writing when you have to work and have a household to care for?" I started believing her. Then to make matters worse, Lady Insecurity became best friends with Mrs. Mom Guilt. They would gang up on me every day. It got so bad that I gave up. I convinced myself I wasn't good enough. Hey, that's the sacrifice you make to be a mom, right? It was normal to put your dreams on hold to give yourself entirely to your family. To a certain extent, I still believe this, but surrendering my dreams wasn't a pill I wanted to swallow. Experiencing life through our child's eyes was teaching me that there were many possibilities in life. If I wanted his dreams to come true, how could I allow my own to fade? I had to teach him never to give up, using myself as an example.

Motherhood wasn't the only thing that affected my thought process when it came to entrepreneurship. Juggling the duties of wife and mom was a strenuous task. It's very much like running a company. There are many working parts to running a household as there is in business. Over time, successfully operating our home like a well-oiled machine gave me the confidence to start my own business. I have not, by any means, perfected how to balance it all. I have come to realize that maintaining relationships with my husband, children, and extended family can be a lot of work. It's essential to organize your time and prioritize. These are the skills you need to possess to run a successful enterprise. My children continue to educate me on patience and time management, LOL. Lord knows moms everywhere are practicing these skills daily. Nurturing, my relationship with my husband is teaching me the importance of providing undivided attention to my spouse. I believe that my relationships with the ones closest to me are helping hone my entrepreneurial skills. Additionally, the most important relationship I have in my life has changed me significantly: My relationship with God.

After eight years of living in my husband's hometown of Philadelphia, I began to yearn for the daily presence of the family that raised me. We had started our own little tribe, but I missed the comforts of my extended family and wanted our son to be able to enjoy them as well. My mother, father, and brother had all journeyed south and took residence in Charlotte, North Carolina. It took some convincing, but my husband eventually agreed to make the trip and move to the Queen City. So, in 2016 this husband, wife and our two wonderful little boys set out to jumpstart our lives in a place very different from where they grew up. We had a game plan to stay with my parents until we purchased a home. I am so glad we did because it was precious time I will always cherish. We bought our first home in spring 2018 and couldn't wait to move in. I imagined big family cookouts and birthday parties. We wanted everything to be perfect, so we started working right away on getting our home prepared, and my father and brother readily pitched in.

The summer of 2018 changed my family forever. On Father's Day, I planned our first family cookout in our home. I was happy that my dad would be able to see what his support had brought us. Still, instead of visiting our house, my father visited the hospital that day. He had been slightly ill for a while but we thought he was getting better. My dad was never a man to get sick often. Growing up as a child, I could barely even remember him having a cold. It was tough to see him in a hospital bed while tubes helped him to breathe. Two days later, he was diagnosed with stage 4 lung cancer. What had begun as the best summer quickly turned to the worst. I struggled with this news and believed that we could help him get better. Unfortunately, three weeks later my father was gone. All the plans involving the whole family came crashing down. Selfishly, I kept asking, 'God, why?! Why would you take him from us now?! We still need him!" My faith in God changed that day. I stopped going to church. I was hurt and angry with God. During the happiest time in my life, someone so special to me was taken. At the time, I couldn't understand God's timing.

After a few months of questioning God, I went back to church. I rededicated my life to God. On my own, I could not find the answers. I decided to seek them from His word even though I wasn't confident in it. I worshipped when I didn't feel like it. I prayed when I wasn't sure if God was listening. My faith was helping me push through. Eventually, I began mourning my earthly father and held onto my faith in the father above. I surrounded myself with other faith-filled people to keep me strong. I always surrounded myself with people of faith to help me move through my grief, but God wasn't done yet. I was still trying to figure out where I belonged in God's plan. I joined an entrepreneurship support group through my church. I was determined to get as much information as I could to help our family reach our business goals. I wanted to make my parents proud. Although my father was no longer with us, I wanted to show him what I was capable of, so I pressed on.

As I began to get my footing back, I stepped into another mental setback. My heart broke again in July of 2019 when I learned that my younger brother was the victim of a deadly car crash. My world began to crumble around me, "God why?! Why would you take him from us now?! We still need him!" I was repeating these same words only a year after my father's passing. I was sure that all the grief that was piling up inside of me would explode, and I would have nothing else to give. I started to wonder if I should even try anymore. Should I set goals for myself? Will it all be in vain? The lives of two of the most influential people in my life were cut short.

I began to question myself again, and Lady Insecurity tried her very best to take root in my heart. She had no problem coaching fear and anxiety into my mind, but I wasn't going to let her win. This time around, I would lean on my faith because I didn't want the pain to rule my life. I'm still in mourning but trying hard to focus on all the joyous memories of my father and brother. It's not easy, and I'm making a conscious decision to let God lead the way. I'm praying that my grief won't get the best of my family and me. I'm praying that we will continue to have high ambitions. I'm praying we'll apply for great jobs and open the businesses of our dreams. I pray we use our pain to prosper. I pray through all of our struggles that our faith will elevate and strengthen us.

Through my suffering, I believe I have found what God intends to do through me. I think the afflictions I have faced forced understanding, faith, and truth. I hope to ascend in my role as a wife, mother, daughter, friend, and future business owner. I will continue to strive to breathe life and love into my artistry and use my talents and passion to help others.

Not that I have already obtained all this, or have already arrived at my goal, but I press on to take hold of that for which Christ Jesus took hold of me. Philippians 3:12 NIV

MY FAITH WALK TO ENTREPRENEURSHIP

Tamra Tolbert-Bush

I remembered the day that I slid the letter across the table to my manager. It read, "I have accepted a position in Charlotte, North Carolina, and will be transferred internally with the bank. Please let this letter serve as my official two weeks' notice."

Luanne looked up at me and smiled. She said, "I am glad that you didn't just accept any old position. You did it the right way. I know you've wanted to move since your mother left for Charlotte a few years ago. I am happy for you, Tamra."

"Thank you," I said. I felt gratitude and anxiety all at once. Putting in my notice somehow solidified things in my mind. Now it was time to start preparing for the transition. I was super excited. *New city, new energy, warmer climate.*

On the other hand, I still had SOMEONE sitting on my shoulders that I had to face. While preparing for my move over the next two weeks, I flashed back to a time long ago, growing up in Buffalo, New York. My roots were there, and my life was blessed. I had never anticipated living anywhere else. To be honest, moving never crossed my mind, until my brother moved to Atlanta and my mother to Charlotte. Buffalo gave me the foundation that I needed to become the compassionate, caring individual that I am today. For this, I thank the Most High God.

One persuasive lesson I have learned from my upbringing is that poverty creates a way of thinking that contributes to violence, crime, and loss of foresight into the future. Who can think about creating a legacy for the generations to come if they cannot rise above their current economic and social crisis? In the community where I am from, so many people struggle. We became comfortable with the dysfunction. I dangerous in so many ways because it determines how we interact with the world around us, what our perception of life is, and how things should be.

Over time I learned that our mindset determines the information we seek, the levels we strive for, and our ability to adapt to change. For these reasons, I gravitated towards corporate America, specifically banking and finance. I wanted to learn about money and the steps I needed to take to bring wealth into my family.

But there was a blip on the route to my smooth transition, my boyfriend. I tried to break up with him multiple times over the years. Something always came up that made me stay. He would cry his eyes out to me every time. Then his grandfather died. Shortly after, his father died. Next, it would be that his children needed me. Or he'd lose another job and have nowhere to go. He would say that no one loved him, but he would threaten to kill himself if I left. There was no end to the excuses he made, and the madness he brought with him.

I allowed him to guilt me into believing that I owed him my life, that I could never leave him. That all I had was him. He made me think that I could trust no one but him: not my family or my friends. In his mind, we would always be together. He wouldn't let me go, and I couldn't break away. It was a never-ending cycle of cheating, lies, manipulation, and psychological and financial abuse. I see that now. I moved to Charlotte, and he followed me six months later.

After months of arguing over the phone, his flight landed in Charlotte. I fell into his trap once again because he promised he was going to find a job and an apartment for us to live in, and I believed him. He needed me to pick him up that morning, so he could use my car for the day while I was at work, to start looking for a job. When I think back, this is where I realized he had my mind. He had never kept or wanted a job in Buffalo, so why would Charlotte be any different? He loved being in the streets. But I agreed. When he picked me up after work, that's when it got crazy.

The officer asked, "Whose name is the car registered to?" We both bolted towards the car in a mad dash. Still, my ex-boyfriend, who shall remain nameless throughout this chapter, arrived first. He snatched the registration out of the glove compartment and hid it before the officer could finish his question.

"It's registered to me!" I shouted. I felt the knot in my throat get bigger, and tears started to roll down my cheeks. I kept looking inside the car as if the registration would magically reappear. "What did you do with it!" I screamed at my ex-boyfriend. "Where is it?"

"It's in there, I don't know what you're talking about," he said with his eyes big and a smirk on his face.

"Officer, he took the registration out and did something with it. This is my car, and it's registered in my name!"

"Well, there is nothing I can do unless I see the registration. You two will have to resolve this among yourselves, I'm sorry, Miss," the officer said.

My ex had taken my car keys and would not give them back. The police did nothing because I was in no immediate physical danger and couldn't prove that it was my car. I was tired, frustrated and angry. I couldn't believe I had allowed myself to get into yet another situation like this. Hadn't I endured enough over the past eleven years of our relationship? I was naïve and stuck on so many levels, both physically and emotionally. I had given this man a full decade of my life, and there were always issues. I had to get away because he was ruining my life, and I knew that God had other plans in store for me.

Fast forward to the late summer of 2007; I had now been living in Charlotte for two years. My transition was successful. I was single, in my new job, with new friends, living my best life. I was also recovering from the scariest time of my life, having been stalked by my ex for a year and a half. That story alone deserves an entire book, but for this chapter, I will just say that I am forever a changed woman because of what I overcame. I learned the value of prayer, awareness, privacy, security, and peace of mind. I realized that the police could not protect me from the terror planted inside my head. Just like in the movies, they always show up after the drama has taken place. That is not a lesson anyone will ever know until they have gone through it.

I also missed out on a blessing because of this situation. A friend of mine offered me a high-level corporate position with the bank. I turned it down from fear of being exposed. I didn't want people to know that I had a crazy person coming after me. GOD used the people around me to break my mental chains of fear eventually. HE awakened me. HE empowered me. Only GOD can give me the tools I need to protect myself. HE saved my life. Hallelujah! I will never let anyone break me down like that again.

We are never tested for the things we claim, we are tested for the things we survive, as the test creates credibility. Tests are temporary. Nothing is permanent except GOD and HIS promises.

- Dr. Myles Monroe

There is no remembrance of former things; neither shall there be any remembrance of things that are to come with those that shall come after. -. Ecclesiastes 1:11

The second half of 2007 was like a dream. I had become settled within the Charlotte social scene while working on my new job. Life was good during this time. I thoroughly enjoyed my single life. I had so much fun that I became pregnant. I linked up with an old friend from my childhood, and the rest is history. So here I was, unmarried and pregnant. Not my ideal situation, but only GOD could judge me. He had blessed me with the gift of life. I simply could not take that for granted. The moment I found out that I was pregnant, I knew that my life would change. I went out on maternity leave two weeks before my scheduled delivery. I gave birth to a strong, healthy baby boy.

While I was on maternity leave in the summer of 2008, it happened. I received a call from my manager, telling me that my position had been eliminated. I was to come back from leave, work for two weeks, and that was it. Legally, they couldn't release me while I was physically on vacation. Ok, fine! Oddly enough, I wasn't upset. But here is the kicker. Two weeks after my last day, my phone rang. I looked at the caller ID, and it was the bank calling me. Spirit said, "Don't answer."

So, I didn't. When I listened to the voice mail, it was my manager calling to ask me to come back to work. Interesting!

My manager called me back again the next day and left another message. I had a new baby and was unemployed, was this my second chance? Spirit still told me clear as day, "Do not answer." I replied, "Ok, LORD, clearly, you have a plan because I surely do not." Anyone in her right mind would have called back to see what their start date was. However, I wasn't in my "own state of mind," I was in "HIS state of mind." HE guided me to go after the opportunity, not the paycheck. My season was about to change, but I didn't know precisely how.

I was grateful to be able to stay at home with my son. But my severance money ran out, and my unemployment was drying up. I had to figure this out. During this time, I found a church home in a small church called God's House of Zion. It wasn't too far from my house, and since I wasn't working outside of the home, I was able to become fully involved in the church. I attended Bible study and other services during the week, in addition to their weekend services. Guest speakers would come in and provide different types of valuable business-oriented information. This was appealing to my mind. It opened me up and completely elevated my way of thinking about money and my future.

One evening in the spring of 2010, I attended a meeting. A woman came in to speak. I won't mention her name. She is a successful entrepreneur in her own right. She talked about personal and business credit. The information blew me away to the point where I was the only one in the room, asking her questions. This was not something they are teaching in schools anywhere in the country. It became a conversation between her and me. I kept raising my hand with more questions, but at the end of the night, that was not enough. I approached her after the meeting to ask if I could come and work for her part-time. She said yes, right on the spot, and we exchanged contact information.

Over the next two months, I was a sponge. I absorbed everything, hanging onto her every word. She assigned me my first client, and I made one thousand dollars in just thirty minutes. My economic psychology had me depending on a job for money, but GOD showed me there was another way. There was a world out there that I knew nothing about. I learned how to educate small businesses and corporations to acquire unsecured lines of credit. I learned how to create private and secure foundations of asset protection using trust as a tool. I had access to a unique, strategic, time-proven, credit building, and lending software. I also helped to restructure businesses to reduce liability and create staying power in their perspective industries. Many of the services she provided were focused on helping small businesses and corporations; In addition to relationship building, vendor alignment, financial literacy, personal credit repair, and mentorship. This experience was amazing. Then I found out she had an emotional disability that made our continued working relationship impossible — two months in, then out.

But GOD is such an awesome GOD. He will give us what we need right when we need it. All of the information I learned was useful information. I did the research myself. I was also validated by other entrepreneurs doing similar work. I had gained a skill that could solve a problem. I continued to build and learn more. I realized that I wanted to do this for myself and leave a legacy to my son. What we learn, we must empty and deposit into the next generation. We must pass the baton. I developed a strong conviction that I could make a valuable contribution to the world, and that I was born because there was something GOD needed me to do. I was sent here to provide information that my generation needs.

In whom also we have obtained an inheritance, being predestinated according to the purpose of him who worketh all things after the counsel of his own will. - Ephesians 1:11 KJV

There is a HUGE informational gap in understanding the keys to life. Many of us will be left following the mindset of the masses, instead of creating our own path. I thank GOD for gifting me with an open mind that was receptive to new information, along with the courage to follow my passion, in HIS name. Amen. As it stands on this day, I am an official online business. I created my business name and begun to brand it in 2014. It took me a while to get going, but I am here now. I needed to be confident and sure of my ability to offer efficient services backed by sustainable data. Now, as a result of the services I provide, I can help people make informed, reasonable financial decisions in their lives.

We currently offer:

· Stock market trading class
· Financial consulting
· Access to secondary Real Estate Tax liens
· Financing
· Business incorporation
· Credit Repair
· Health and life insurance
· Trust preparation
· Surplus recovery
· Grant Writing

THE LORD IS MY SHEPHERD

Belinda Spears

"The LORD is my Shepherd; I shall not want." (Psalms 23:1).

Life is full of twists and turns. Sometimes our dreams come true. Sometimes we end up wondering how we got in this mess. As trials and tribulations have come my way, I have learned to hold fast to God's unchanging hand. I'm a Faith Entrepreneur, and I desire to build up lives through godly short stories. I consider it an honor to work alongside my sisters and brothers in Christ to expand the Kingdom of God. I have fallen several times, but the LORD is still my Shepherd. He has watched over me, loved me through the good and the bad. However, some things I brought on myself due to disobedience let me share with you.

One dreary afternoon, it was pouring down rain. There were thick grayish clouds, accompanied by strong winds. My husband was driving me to work, and my toddler son was sitting in the backseat. We had just approached the bridge on highway 16. All of a sudden, the car hydroplaned, skidding into the metal bars on the passenger side where I was sitting. I hollered and began applying imaginary brakes on my side, in

51

vain. My seatbelt could not contain me as the force from the crash planted my face into the dashboard. I felt no pain as my spirit drifted outside of my body. I envisioned my physical self climbing in the clouds towards heaven, quoting The 23rd Psalm.

"1.The LORD is my Shepherd; I shall not want. 2.He maketh me to lie down in green pastures: He leadeth me beside the still waters. He restoreth my soul. He leadeth me in the paths of righteousness for His name's sake. 4Yea, though I walk through the valley of the shadow of death, I will fear no evil: for thou art with me; thy rod and thy staff they comfort me. 5Thou preparest a table before me in the presence of mine enemies: Thou anointest my head with oil; my cup runneth over. 6Surely goodness and mercy shall follow me all the days of my life: and I will dwell in the house of the LORD forever."

I repeated the 23rd Psalm from beginning to end several times. The higher I climbed, the sky cleared, the rain stopped. Before I reached my destination, I heard the medical personnel open the passenger door. The cold air hit my face, and my eyes popped open. I was back in my body, trying to move. The medic told me to be still. I tasted blood as I attempted to speak. What about my baby? I was informed that my son had a lot of cracked glass on him, but he was perfectly fine, without a scratch. While my husband received bruises and scratch marks, I sustained most of the injuries. I had to get the roof of my mouth stitched up and learn how to eat again. My nose got scratched and bruised. It was swollen. I had difficulty breathing. I had to use oxygen for a couple of days in the hospital. The doctor ruled out my nose being broken; however, it felt painful to touch. My lower extremities were messed up, and I had to learn to walk again. We all went to the emergency room to be checked out. I had to be admitted. Upon being released, one of my sisters took me to her home to nurse me back to health.

The experience wasn't easy for either of us, but God carried us through. Great is His faithfulness. He is a good Shepherd that will pick us up and carry us when we are not able.

God's word says, "Lo, I am with you always, even till the end of the earth." I am a witness to this truth. He hasn't failed me yet. When I was a child, I remember being asleep, with my right arm hanging out of bed. I woke up screaming to a mouse chewing on my index finger. Mommy and Daddy took me to the hospital to get a tetanus shot. For a very long time, I had to look at an ugly scar from the mouse bite on my finger each day, which eventually cleared up in adulthood. That scar was likely a metaphor for my painful childhood. I didn't get to be a kid for long because I had major responsibility for my siblings as the oldest. Although I had quite a bit on me, I liked being in charge. I was quiet, but I spoke up when I had to.

When I turned 18, I started working part-time. My parents taught me to work hard and to do my best. I had to set the example for my two brothers and five sisters, plus put money aside for college. I remember being sleepy and tired a lot, but I was motivated by my momma to keep striving. She encouraged me to push past the discomfort because breakthrough was around the corner. "Many times in this world," she'd say, "one will have peace one minute, then storms will come. Life is not without thorns, but it will become what you make it. So be wise in making your decisions while in it." During my struggles between juggling school, my job, and my responsibilities at home, I kept her words in mind. I also always kept the 23rd Psalm close to my heart. The LORD has been my Shepherd all the way.

Something else happened after I turned 18. I felt the desire to attend church. My siblings and I were raised on the Word of God at home, not in the church. Why? Because my father stated, church people were hypocrites! Something inside me wanted to be around others in Christ, so I asked Daddy if I could go. He said yes, so a lady in my neighborhood took me to church regularly. I gave my life to Jesus while in church. Within a couple of weeks, I was water baptized. Instantly, I felt clean inside. I wasn't expecting anything from God; I only wanted to be obedient to what I heard God saying within my spirit. I will forever be grateful to my father for the background he established in my siblings and me. We used to memorize scriptures, and we would have our own "Sunday Service" at home. We found out later in life that Daddy used to be a "Street Minister," saving souls and preaching to the common man. This probably explains why he was suspicious of church people who he felt didn't do enough to reach those outside of church walls. However, he never stood in the way of God's calling to others in our family into the ministry.

At the age of 21, I finished college with nursing credentials. I moved into my own apartment with a roommate. To celebrate, I booked an appointment at Belk's Department Store for a beauty product consultation. I felt like an adult, grown-up, and pretty. So I took a picture, a memento of that day and time. God had brought me so far, "The LORD is my Shepherd!" I had no idea what my future had in store. Still, within my soul, I knew the LORD watches over the sparrow. Therefore, I knew He would do the same for me.

During my nursing career, I encountered a patient who was about to commit suicide. Her goal was to end her life by jumping out of the window. I didn't know what to do. I was in charge that night. I called on Jesus for help silently. I sent someone to call for the Supervisor. I remained calm on the outside and listened to her story. She indicated life was too painful. Things weren't right in her world, and nothing was worth fighting for. She was tired and ready to throw in the towel. Finally, I encouraged her to give life another try. I told her to focus on the good and put it in God's hands, that He will help her to make it. At some point, things will get better. I encouraged her to trust God. Her situation may have been too big for her, but it was just right for God. She hugged me, but we still moved her to another unit where she could be closely monitored. I'm so glad God gave me the words to be able to convey to that young woman what I had been taught and had observed my whole life. God spoke to me, and I talked to her. If nothing else, I was able to comfort her raging mind. "Yea, though I walk through the valley of the shadow of death, I will fear no evil: for thou art with me; thy rod and thy staff they comfort me."

The Lord wants the best for us. If He says don't get involved in things, He means it. When I was younger, I wanted everything to go my way. I was disobedient with the Lord and ended up in a marriage that resulted in a separation and, later, a divorce. There are always two sides to a story in a bad relationship. My story was that I was verbally and physically abused. In the beginning, I did not follow the advice of loved ones who advised me not to marry my husband. Others had said he was not my soulmate, but I was blinded by love. My husband even informed me that he was not interested in marrying me as we got closer to our wedding date. I saw all the red flags of rejections from him. Still, because I had invested money in a gown, bridesmaid dresses, etc., I personally decided to continue with the wedding. Most importantly, I was pregnant and was using our baby as an ultimatum to try and keep him. It worked. We got married, and he was happy when our baby boy was born.

I thought our baby would make him love me more, but it did not. I can tell because he was not showing affection, such as holding my hand or doing loving things with me. And then, things changed for the worse. One night, he came home drunk. I was putting our son to bed as he staggered into the house, bumping into furniture. Drunk out of his mind, he chased and attacked me. He physically abused me. His actions that night became a pattern throughout our marriage and turned into a crisis for our family. Those traumatic experiences affected my young son and me for a long time. God carried me through those horrible times in my marriage, but it could have been avoided if I had been obedient from the beginning. After I found my strength and courage, I left my husband and my son, and I ended up in a shelter for a short while. I called my middle sister, and she took us in until I saved up enough money to move to an apartment.

After the divorce, I was interested in making extra money. I found I liked experimenting with entrepreneurial efforts such as starting businesses. One of the businesses I started involved buying and re-selling items. Both of my brothers took me to places where an individual could buy bulk supplies. Everything there was sold "as is." I invested money with them. We bought musical instruments; pianos, typewriters, nine keys, and other types of clerical equipment. My brothers refurbished the items for profit, and I helped with the bookkeeping. We ended up breaking even, no profit. Thankfully, only our own money was used; there was no loan involved. Despite not making a profit, this proved to be an excellent learning experience. In addition to the money we invested, we also invested two years of our time. Hoping for success, we analyzed our data and organized our workload. Everybody worked together to accomplish set goals. Once we realized we weren't going to be making a huge profit, we decided to sell what was left for a reasonable price to recoup our initial monetary investment. We realized our business didn't work due to a lack of a business plan. I continued to thank God because it could have turned out a lot worse.

Our next business venture came about when my youngest brother designed a garbage can. Perhaps I should have learned from the previous business failure, but obviously, I like to take risks. Besides, I read the blueprint. I examined and tested the mini model. It looked realistic and effective. It was almost, if not similar, to garbage cans at nursing homes. So, I decided to invest $350.00 towards the project. We paid for the patent, and he connected with a friend of his in New York. The guy took all our money, we never saw him again. A big loss! There was no way to reach him; he disappeared. Another lesson learned: There should have been a legal contract in place. I was really hurt. I cried a little, but I got over it thanks to my faith and the 23rd Psalm. "Thou preparest a table before me in the presence of mine enemies: Thou anointest my head with oil; my cup runneth over."

I have learned from mistakes. It's okay to fall, just don't stay down, get back up, and try again. After all, God is checking out how we handle issues that He allows in our lives. Will we freak out, spinning our wheels, or will we ask Him for help and figure out how to put the pieces back together?

Lastly, I participated in several multi-level marketing businesses. I sold designer wall prints, Mary Kay, and clothes. I had fun doing it, but I realized this wasn't for me. Today, I feel like I've learned so much from my business experiences. I tend to talk things over more thoroughly with family. I always create a business plan. No matter the venture, everything is always placed in order. In life, I have learned that everything works together for our good and is based on God's plan and purpose for our lives.

The pain from the separation and divorce of my marriage, along with other disappointments in my life, led me to write short prayers and skits based on scriptures. God allowed me to use this gift of writing to inspire and uplift others by sharing my personal experiences. God led me to where I am now as an educator and a minister. Along the way, I have discovered my purpose. I desire to impact people's lives by encouraging transformation in their hearts. Within the right season, under the Lord's guidance, I will create short stories that will fill hearts with joy, love, and help individuals to make good choices in life.

We all can touch lives every day, by a smile or helping hand. We are here to make a difference in someone's life. We can look to the example of Jesus to show us how. The Lord is our Shepherd all day long. I hope my story will encourage you on your journey. All it takes is one first step.

IT TAKES A TEAM

Casey C. Ifedi

It was my freshman year in college at East Carolina University. I was a wide-eyed eighteen-year-old with a world of optimism and opportunity in full view. I had traveled over two hundred and fifty miles to try this college thing out. After a chaotic day, I sat on my bed and went over the events in my head. I drifted off, but before I could fall asleep, I felt a slight vibration, it was my phone. Groggy, I answered. It was Chris.

"Hello Gen, did you hear what happened?" Chris asked.

"What are you talking about?" I said. "Jerome is dead! He and his baby's mother's brother were arguing earlier that day. Jerome went to Bible study, and on his walk back home, the brother shot and killed him on the spot! No communication, no reasoning, he just let shots out and sped off." "Are you serious?" I yelled into the phone, disbelieving. I quickly cut the call and drove straight to the gym to work out what just took place. Jerome is dead? Not Jerome Tank, there is no way! I believed I stayed in the gym that night for about 4 hours.

As a first-generation Nigerian-American child in America, we were heavily sheltered. We were not allowed to play outside with the neighborhood kids. Jerome was the first neighborhood

61

kid that we had the opportunity to play with and develop a relationship. Milton Road provided a sense of community, a brotherhood, family dedication and pride. August 3, 2010 would mark a personal shift and change in my life. This death hit close to home — a brother, a soldier, shot in plain sight. Within a blink of an eye - a life, a son, a father, a family was changed forever. Instead of reasoning and communicating as men, the first response was violence. At this point, I had more questions than answers. Who can we blame for this loss? Should we blame the government, society, or the system which enables perpetual self-hate and indifference? Ultimately, I decided that the only person I could hold accountable for what had occurred in my community was myself. I must be the change I want to see in this world.

The death of my dear friend pushed my life to a purpose. From that moment forward, I decided to take a stand against disunity, indifference, mediocrity, and poverty of the mind. Starting with myself, I would become a talented, empowered, aspiring man, part of a T.E.A.M. I would inspire other men to do the same. I promised Jerome in heaven that I would spread this message to the world. Maybe if every man aspired to be on the T.E.A.M., I could help stop men from killing other men. Even though I was just a freshman, I jumped out on faith to start and register T.E.A.M. as a campus organization. To register an organization on campus, a student must find a responsible faculty/staff advisor who will act as a liaison between the student body and the university.

We believed we had found a person that fit those requirements. I reached out to the advisor to see if he would be on board to help move our mission and goals forward. After a candid meeting, the advisor agreed to partner with us. The T.E.A.M. and I were excited to have a university staff member endorse our cause.

During the inaugural semester, we planned and strategically networked. We worked to create a flawless game plan that could stand the test of time. Our first major program was titled: The T.E.A.M. vs. Breast Cancer Talent Showcase. Every T.E.A.M. member had been affected by breast cancer in some way. The T.E.A.M. vs. Breast Cancer would serve as a fundraiser for breast cancer research. The event would be a talent showcase open to the community. Talent showcases create an opportunity for organizations around campus to come together. We would do our part to help find the cure for a disease that had taken so many of our dear loved ones. Many of our members were honored to participate in such a noble and personal cause. As The T.E.A.M. vs. Breast Cancer program drew closer, we were really pushed and tested from all sides.

Many campus fraternities and organizations were not pleased that we were working on an event that would unite the university community. One particular group went as far as promising their support and attendance only to detract later and dismiss the entire cause and mission of breast cancer awareness. The pressure started to worry some of the members. As the leader of this prestigious and forward-thinking group, I held myself responsible for the success or failure of our organization. As the challenges and tests of our inaugural semester started to increase, I reached out to our campus advisor. I called, emailed, and texted the advisor on several occasions in order to receive advice and instructions on how to navigate this new terrain. He never responded.

Since we were unable to connect with our campus advisor, I decided to call an emergency meeting. The T.E.A.M. vs. Breast Cancer talent showcase was less than a week out, and we still needed slots filled, T.E.A.M. gear ordered, and a printed itinerary with all of the acts and their information. In short, with less than a week until the program, we were up against a challenge. Typically I am the big brother that my family and friends can come to whenever they need any advice from a male's perspective, so I figured I had better rise to the occasion and made sure the organization that was near and dear to my heart did not fail.

I can generally handle many responsibilities and generally wear multiple hats at one time. For the first time, I found myself inadequate to manage this coming challenge alone. I had to face myself and be brutally honest. This challenge would take more than me. It would take a team or a T.E.A.M. of individuals working together as one. With our goal in mind, we would have to creatively approach the problem using our varied perspectives and vantage points. I looked at my brothers and T.E.A.M. members squarely in the face, and I let them know that I needed them to step up now.

"The leaders of this organization have carried the torch as far as we can individually," I said. "Today, we must awaken the lion inside. No longer can we take a backseat as we fight for humanity. You, too, must pick up your cross and stand for truth." During the meeting, each T.E.A.M. member was required to head at least one committee. It did not matter which task was taken up as long as the member took ownership of their assignment. At that time, we had roughly twenty members. Out of those twenty members, about six of those members were one hundred percent committed to our organization's mission and goals. As we broke up The T.E.A.M. into smaller teams, we realized that each member became increasingly motivated and committed not only to themselves but to one another.

During this process, our university advisor quit on us. He did not believe we could make the event happen, and even suggested that we should turn our attention away from the T.E.A.M. vs. Cancer Talent Showcase and focus on starting an intramural basketball team. As the event approached, we invited the vice-chancellor to the event. After weeks of follow up, we realized she too was not interested in our organization's mission and overall goal. We were disappointed to learn that The T.E.A.M. vs. Cancer talent showcase would not be backed or supported by any university official. We were tired of the lack of leadership. We decided the only leaders that could run and operate this organization would be us. With just days ahead, a game plan was created and mapped out.

D.J. would be responsible for the overall stage sound and the music of each act. Jordan would follow up with the acts to ensure that they attend rehearsals and would be prepared for the event. Charles was in charge of communicating and emailing vendors, acts, and university officials any necessary updates as the event approached. Will and Leo took on promotion and advertisement for the event. Jamine and I were responsible for organizing the event and ensuring every committee fulfilled their assigned role and task. We were also responsible for the necessary paperwork that was needed.

After weeks of preparation before the exit of our advisor and several sleepless nights once we learned he would not be assisting us, the day was upon us. The night prior, I was unable to sleep adequately. I started to become a little restless, and then I heard a low, quiet, but peaceful voice speak to me. One simple phrase continued to repeat and surround me as I tried to drift off "Peace be still; I am with you." As I heard these words, I felt the stress of the burden and pressure I was facing begin to fade and become a lot more bearable.

I woke up the next morning, prepared to execute our plan. I walked up to the members to encourage them and to assure them that today will be a success. "The day of the event will mark the beginning of our destiny," I said.

We made time to schedule a quick run-through with each act. It was to be a kind of dress rehearsal with each act running through their proposed performance. We expected about five to seven acts actually to show up, but to our surprise, thirteen acts arrived to practice. I was overwhelmed by the amount of support and appreciation for each act displayed. One particular act left a lasting impression on me. Justin was a talented singer and piano player. As Justin walked in, he came up to us. He told us how much he appreciated the opportunity to perform for such a personal cause for him. He then went on to say to us that he had recently lost a loved one from breast cancer and would be honored to do his part to find the cure for the disease. At that moment, I realized that the work we were doing was more significant than any one of us.

As I looked around, I was amazed to see how diligent each member was working. Everyone understood what was at stake. As we rounded up our last rehearsals before the big day, an older gentleman walked in. He had a surprised and baffled look on his face. As I walked closer, I realized that it was our advisor. I asked him, "What are you doing here?" "I've come to oversee your operation to make sure there aren't any issues." He looked around, seemingly surprised by the activity and organization in his sight. "Thank you, sir. We are good," I said. "We reached out to you on several occasions over the course of the month, but we felt like you weren't interested in offering any assistance or advice during our process. Remember, you suggested we drop the showcase altogether and put together intramural basketball." I could tell he seemed taken aback by my response. "Don't worry," I continued. "We realized we truly are the leaders of this organization, and after our event, we will look for another university advisor that clearly understands our goals and mission." I watched him look around the room and make a hasty retreat. I shrugged my shoulders as the other members shot me questioning glances.

October 17, 2012, finally arrived on the calendar. I woke up excited and appreciative that the event we planned for six months was less than 24 hours away. I thanked God for the opportunity to pursue my purpose and then went outside for a quick workout. After the workout, I went back upstairs to my room to shower and prepare. My brother Jordan picked me up, and then we drove to the event. Once there, we had a quick meeting with all of the T.E.A.M. members. I told them that I appreciated them and that through this process, I discovered true leaders.

"If you look to your right and left, you will see a man that did not give up. I am proud of each of you all. During this process, I learned what teamwork means. I could not have made the event happen without you, gentlemen. I am a better man, brother, son, and leader because of you all." I stood in the circle we had formed and looked at each man in the eye. I noticed how each man had changed. Everyone looked more accomplished and more confident than they had six months before. "I never believed that I could lead or operate an organization of this size prior to this season. Regardless of what happens today, I want you each to know and understand that you are winners. You started something, and you finished. I thank God for your lives." We had truly become members of a T.E.A.M.

The T.E.A.M. vs. Cancer talent showcase was a huge success. In total, 15 acts performed, and the students and administration were inspired and enthused. I moderated the event, and I instantly fell in love with the microphone that day. Each act came out and left everything on the stage. We had singers, rappers, poets, musicians, and even an opera singer. It was time for us to wrap up the event, but the people refused to leave.

After each act, I would present an interesting fact about breast cancer. One fact that caught people off guard was that men could also have breast cancer. That one statement created a conversation that would progress even outside of the event. We were able to collect just under 2 thousand dollars from our showcase, bracelets, and collaborative efforts. I thanked everyone for coming out and closed the event with our signature song. "It takes a T.E.A.M.; are you rolling with The T.E.A.M.? It takes a T.E.A.M.!"

I was so grateful for the opportunity to memorialize my friend Jerome in a way that led to success for our new campus organization, T.E.A.M. I feel like we made a difference by helping to organize an event that funded a cause that had meaning for all of us. We didn't realize it at the time, but we participated in what could be called, systematized collaboration. We leveraged our talents and came together in a pinch. I can only hope that Jerome is smiling down on us, knowing his life encouraged others to make a positive difference.

HOPE DEFFERED BUT SUSTAINED BY FAITH

Stephanie Morris

Faith is a course of action. It is faith that creates outcomes.

Hope deferred makes the heart sick, but when dreams come true at last, there is life and joy. - Proverbs 13:12 (The Living Bible)

Hope is a feeling of expectation and desire for a sure thing to happen. The word deferred means to put off to a later time, postpone. When what you are hoping for, dreaming for, looking for, or asking for does not materialize over time; you may become ill, sad, disappointed, disgusted, frustrated, angry, lost, or all of the above. Hope deferred can be paralyzing. As a matter of fact, hope deferred can lead to a state of depression. You isolate yourself and lose the will to live. You give up on your dreams, and everything looks dark and hopeless. Even for a person of faith, it can often lead us away from prayer and trusting in God. Unfortunately, it can be an open door for Satan to creep in and speak lies into our minds. For some, deferred hope may mean desiring a child but not being able to conceive, not getting a job or promotion you feel you deserve or persistent health problems.

71

For me, hope deferred pertained to all my attempts to build a successful business while not seeing the fruit from my efforts. Hope deferred, but I am sustained by my faith. When you are a person of strong faith, being connected to God the creator of all things means the challenges that you go through will be a vehicle of growth, not demise. How you handle your challenges, disappointments, and failures is what is most important. As a woman of faith, I will not give up on my dreams, and I will continue to pray and ask God for His fresh anointing and direction. I will ask Him to renew my mind and to give me a divine strategy to implement for my businesses.

My journey to entrepreneurship has not been easy or totally fulfilling for my spirit or bank account. I'm eight years into my journey as a full-time entrepreneur, and I still wonder if I have what it takes. After years of investing money into real estate education and coaching, I ask myself what else is needed to get ahead. Frustrated, confused, disillusioned, disappointed, distraught are the feelings that consume me in this season. How on earth did I find myself HERE, ready to give up on my dreams, purpose, and life? In the darkness of failed businesses and dreams, the thought of throwing it all to the wind and getting a full-time job preoccupy my mind daily. *Hope deferred but sustained by faith.*

My career as a full-time entrepreneur began eight years ago when my twenty-two-year career ended. My optimism led me to the next phase of my life of building a real estate empire. My passion for real estate investing was peaked in my early thirties when I attended a workshop on how to get started in real estate without any money. The concept sounded easy, and the money that was being made by these real estate "experts/gurus" was attractive. They made it look so simple. The crazy thing is the courses/coaching was not cheap. I did not realize this would spiral into a five-year journey of investing thousands of dollars on education. As an information junkie, I attended every real estate boot camp, workshop, and seminar, I could find to learn every real estate strategy that was out there. The only thing is I never applied what I learned.

Key Lesson #1: Investing money in learning without doing the work will not bring you success.

All hard work brings a profit, but mere talk leads only to poverty. ~Proverbs 14:23-24

You can talk all day every day about your dreams and plans, but if you do not put income-producing activities into your daily action plan, you will not reap a reward, you will only remain poor. As I worked my business as a real estate investor, I realized I had many fears that kept me paralyzed from taking action. I lacked confidence in my ability to talk to distressed homeowners and to execute a deal. However, I found a great support system when I joined a real estate investor association.

It was through this connection that I learned about a "Done For You" model of investing. I loved this model because it consisted of a team of professionals that guided me in the acquisition of a property. It was through this model that I purchased my first rental property.

Key Lesson #2: You need to find a team of professional people "experts" to believe in you and support you in overcoming your fears.

Iron sharpens iron, and one man sharpens another. ~Proverbs 27:17 (English Standard Version)

It is essential in life and business to have people that will hold you accountable and to support you in your dreams. Not everyone will understand your purpose, your message, or your drive for success. I know we all want our family and friends to support and believe in our dreams, but they are often not the ones to see your potential and be your cheerleader. I have found that people who do not know you personally tend to be the most supportive. It is crucial to find a mentor or coach who does understand and can guide you and propel you toward achieving your goal.

Although I purchased my first rental property, I still struggled on the investment side of real estate. Instead, I decided to get my license as a real estate agent, and after three tough and frustrating years of working as an agent, I thought a change of environment would help me at this stage in my journey. I felt that my promised land was not in New York, so I moved to North Carolina. This was a leap of faith, and I trusted God to "work a miracle."

My plan was to get a job and an apartment. I also planned to re-launch my real estate investing career in NC with a partner. Our first month in NC, my partner saw a house for sale but had been under contract for a full month. After the month was over, the realtor called her and asked if she wanted to see the house. We walked into the house, and I instantly fell in love with it. I wanted it for myself to live in, not to fix to rent or resell. I put in an offer, and it was accepted. Yes, you are reading this correctly. No job, but I purchased a house. But GOD!!! Let me share that I had retirement money and was able to purchase it with cash. God led me into this house because I honestly had no intention of buying a home. Remember, my plan was to get a job and an apartment.

Key Lesson # 3: God will guide your steps once you start taking them.

We must learn to take action despite any distractions! How can God guide you if you are sitting still? As a believer, I continue to lean on the word of God. I know many of us are "waiting on God" to show us our purpose or how to take action on our dreams. I learned that God is waiting on ME to have faith enough to take action without knowing the full outcome. I do remember at a real estate appointment in NY when the homeowner was an acquaintance of my friend; God whispered in my spiritual ear, "See, I make things easy." God can connect us to resources and people that will help us fulfill our goals.

For I know the plans I have for you," declares the Lord, "plans to prosper you and not to harm you, plans to give you hope and a future. Then you will call on me and come and pray to me, and I will listen to you. You will seek me and find me when you seek me with all your heart. ~Jeremiah 29:11-13

That was three years ago, and now today, sitting in my "Happy Place" I am still uncomfortable because not all of my dreams have materialized. Yes, I closed on my house and another rental property, but for some reason, I still feel stuck. I realize entrepreneurship is not easy because everything falls on your shoulders. If money is not coming in, then you do not have any to pay bills or medical expenses. You must market your services consistently and attract new clients/customers. Sometimes it is lonely if you work at home. Also, thoughts of how people view your success may plague your mind. Being responsible for every aspect of a business can be draining. In this season, God is refreshing my spirit and mind. I have a renewed hope to continue to build my business in real estate. God did not say we would not have any challenges, problems, or struggles. What he said was He will never leave us nor forsake us in those struggles.

Make sure that your character is free from the love of money, being content with what you have; for He, Himself has said, "I will never desert you, nor will I ever forsake you," ~Hebrews 13:5 (New American Standard Bible)

As I continue to seek the Lord, He continues to give me the desires of my heart. I realize that my life is a faith walk and that as long as I hold onto the promises of God, seeking Him to direct my path, He will continue to reward my efforts to build a kingdom business that will serve the marketplace.

Take delight in the Lord, and he will give you the desires of your heart. Commit your way to the Lord; trust in him and he will do this: He will make your righteous reward shine like the dawn, your vindication like the noonday sun. ~ Psalm 37:4-6 (New International Version.)

God has placed a mission for seniors in my heart. I know I am to serve the seniors with housing, transportation, and to help them reconnect to their worth. Some people have a heart for children; some for young adults, mine is for the older generation. Our seniors have weathered many storms and have so much knowledge to give. I recognize that as they have lived through the season of raising children, retired from their careers; they may find themselves in a state of hope deferred. They could be lonely, unfulfilled, and wondering what is next? How could I be of use in my old age? Well, God still has a purpose for our older generation, and it is my goal to help them share their value in whatever form God will reveal.

My real estate journey is far from over; I am forming a new company that will find properties for seniors. God has given me a new resource, which is like the ram in the bush. I am so excited about the new venture. My goal is to partner with someone who will share the workload and provide support. I know God will supply the necessary resources that will help me to fulfill my dreams. As a "Kingdom Driven Entrepreneur," sometimes it is needed to take some time to get still and regroup. I have prayed and asked God to refresh my dreams and to allow me to re-invent my business.

Key Lesson #4: Never give up. Ask God to give you the strength to tackle your fears. Ask God to give you the courage to step out in faith to live your purpose. You can Do It!

I can do all things through Christ who strengthens me.
~Philippians 4:13 (New King James Version)

My message to you is, "Never give up!" Continue to lean into God, He sees you, He knows you. Most importantly, God LOVES YOU! You are needed to bring Heaven into this earth realm. My daily prayer is for God to use me so that I can make a difference in someone's life. My hope may be deferred, but not for long as I continue to have FAITH. I will shine my little light as bright as I can because I am an overcomer. Although I am still working and walking my kingdom entrepreneurship journey, I stand on the word of God. I am sustained by my faith "that which is not seen but will soon become my reality."

Now faith is the substance of things hoped for, the evidence of
things not seen. ~Hebrews 11:1(King James Version)

SDM Connection Enterprises, LLC is my business that will provide coaching to help people discover their passion and take action to fulfill their purpose, through vision boards and goal-setting workshops. It is my goal to build my kingdom business so that people will see the attributes of God. SDM Connection Enterprises, LLC shines brightly in the marketplace, known for exceptional customer service, integrity, fairness, and excellent business practices.

Let your light so shine before men, that they may see your good works and glorify your Father in heaven. ~Matthew 5:16 (New King James Version)

.

E.S.C.A.P.E to Charlotte

Rene' T. Brewer

I have always known that my life would be a testimony. What I wasn't aware of is what I had to go through for this testimony to manifest. As a young child, I consistently talked about what I wanted to do in life, how I would do it, and where I would do it. I had it all planned out as it constantly changed. My daddy, a wonderful husband, and father of eight used to say, I can't wait to see you do what you say you will do because you are my child who is always dreaming.

I could be found on any given day with my head in a book because, in a book, I was an only child, not the fifth of eight. In a book, I would see myself as the character exploring with no limitations. I went to school with a desire to be a teacher or a psychologist. Mental health won. Once out of college, I decided that I was going to leave Chicago and go to San Diego, California! I was going there to teach and receive my Masters; all signs pointed to the West Coast.

Before Cali, my life took a different route. At 26 years old, I had my son, but California was still my destination. I requested information and applications from various schools. I researched educational requirements to teach and the cost of living out there. But after my daughter was born when I turned 28, I realized that Cali was no longer an option. I began working at a center as a youth worker for students in the after-school program. This was one of the most rewarding jobs I ever had the pleasure of working. I remember my first day going into this building, unaware but ready. And of course, on my first day, I got tried. I'll never forget what happened when I asked this one young man to do his homework, and he had no issue telling me what he was not going to do. He proceeded to walk menacingly toward me as if he was threatening one of his friends. I calmly stated to him, "There will be two hits if you walk upon me: Me hitting you and you hitting the floor." He yelled, "Teachers can't hit students." I told him, "Today is your lucky day because I am not a teacher." This was the incident that gained me my respect! I had no problems with disrespect after that encounter.

Six months of being at the center and building relationships, I decided I no longer wanted to teach inside a classroom, sitting behind a desk, creating impersonal relationships with the children that I worked with. I desired to give them more. My babies at that center not only poured into me, but they also allowed me to pour into them. We had more heart to heart group talks than anything else. I enjoyed the emotional bonding, and it became heavy at times. Working with the youth on this level gave me a new perspective. I had never sat down with youth with "real stressors," such as youth who attempted suicide, had parents on drugs, parents that didn't care about them, or youth who had never ventured outside of their neighborhood. As they continued to come to the center, I realized these children were unlike the average teens with baggage. I enjoyed working with both the males and the females; however, I enjoyed watching the girls increase their self-awareness and self-worth as they gained an understanding of who and what they represent as African-American young women.

Were there times that I doubted my contribution to the lives of these young people? Yes! My pregnancy with my daughter was one of those times when I felt like I had failed them. I remember feeling anxious and depressed as I asked myself, how can you preach to these teens about safe, protected sex, and then get pregnant! I believe my disappointment in myself led me to think that they would be disappointed in me as well. I stood before them apologizing for being a hypocrite for asking them to do something that I, as a grown woman, did not do. Their response was priceless as they assured me that they saw me no different because we all make mistakes. Can we say instant tears?

While I was out on maternity leave, I thought about how much wisdom I had gained working with teens and how my guidance had changed so many lives. One of my male students told me upon my return that he honestly missed me because I provided for him a structure that he did not get at home. I will never forget his words, "Ms. Brewer, we like to be told what to do because it means you care." Who would've thought?

I applied for graduate school in Chicago while also submitting paperwork to become a homeowner. Denied for both, I was beginning to feel a bit defeated, and as I sat in my feelings, I heard, *start a mentoring group for girls.* I whispered my reply, "Really, Lord? Ok, that I can do." No sooner had I decided that a mentoring group was something doable, God said, "Not here." I had lived in Chicago my entire life. I went 45mins away to college and missed my siblings terribly. My father had not too long passed away, and I needed them, and my mom even more now.

I could not understand why God's plan did not sound anything like my books or what I had been telling myself I wanted, but I began to get an idea as to why nothing was coming together for me. My daughter was born two years after my son, and yes, I still hadn't moved because I didn't know how to proceed. My desire was to be obedient, but what did that look like with no direction? I didn't realize that I was already moving in that direction.

When I turned 31, God informed me it was time to move. The location was yet to be revealed to me, but in my spirit, there was peace. My brother- in- law's brother had lived in Charlotte, NC for years and as we sat at my brother's house one afternoon during one of his visits, his wife plainly stated, "Why don't you

84

move to Charlotte? We're a little slower and quieter than what you're used to, but nice." And bam, there it was! Was Charlotte the place where God needed and wanted me?

I have never prayed so much for confirmation, because why would God move me away from my mommy and siblings? Other than that 45min ride to college, I had never been away from them. My two older sisters had gone off into military life and were the only ones that had really ventured out of the nest, but even they came back home. I had one other sibling that went out of state for college, but he also returned; we think maybe it was separation anxiety. My family revitalizes me. They give me energy, hope, and peace, reminding me that I am loved; we enjoy being around each other.

In 2007, I remembered telling my sister-in-love (sister by marriage) that seven was the year of completion and that God was telling me that it was time. I continued to hear my grandmother's voice from years prior, as she called me to her side in that hospital room to inform me that God was ready to use me to do great things and that I had to be open to allow him to use me. I also thought back to the time my mom and I had done a girl's getaway. As she held me, she told me she remembered God spoke to her and said that He would use me and that I was created for greatness. Now here I was nervous and excited about moving towards greatness. I immediately jumped into action looking up apartments, applying for jobs, and saving money.

The one thing I did not do was inform my mother of my plans to move. Telling mommy made it real, and I wasn't ready for the move to be real. Wow, as I type this, the emotions resurface. This journey that I was embarking on, this God-led journey was about my children and me. I had never really been on my own because I've always had my family, my support, the other part that made me who I am. After numerous confirmations, I was mentally, spiritually, and emotionally ready to go. However, I still had not told my mom. On Christmas day, 2007, my mom gave me a card, and as always, she wrote a personal note inside with her favorite scripture: *Trust in the Lord with all thine heart; and lean not unto thy own understanding but in all thy ways acknowledge him and he shall direct thy path.* Proverbs 3:5-6. KJV. She also told me to be obedient to where God leads me to go because wherever I go, God will use me. That encouraging Christmas card was the final confirmation that my time had come. Why? Because nobody else had informed my mom of my decision to move, yet her card seemed to bless the move that she knew nothing about. Let me tell you when I say God worked that thing!

A job came along via one person in North Carolina that knew four people in Chicago that I knew, but they didn't know each other. By June 2008, I had a job and a place to stay. By August 2008, Charlotte became my new home. I ventured into North Carolina with great anticipation, wondering what's next. I was a single mom with a six and three-year-old, waiting for direction. My first job in Charlotte was a Foster Care Case Manager for Sexually Aggressive Youth. This job was not only mentally and emotionally challenging; it was spiritually challenging as well. Sometimes dealing with the children was better than dealing with some of the people in the office. One lady and her partner in crime in Human Resources were on a mission to see me leave the agency. They would do things like go on my computer when I wasn't there to see if the history was work-related. They started a sign in and out sheet to time how long I was out of the office with clients. They'd change paperwork and do just about anything to ensure my stay wasn't permanent.

One day as I sat at my desk in tears from frustration, one of the foster parents came in and said to me, Rene', my wife is in the car, and she needs to talk with you. The minute my backside touched the car seat, the tears flowed. His wife, who was also a pastor, looked at me and simply stated, "Rene', God is about to move you from this place, there is a spiritual warfare going on here that you are not equipped to fight." Mind-Blowing moment! Three days later, God confirmed to me that I would be let go by the end of the week. I had no idea what was next, but I accepted his word and waited. This is where it gets interesting. The transition from employed to unemployed took place in February 2009. God had given me a six-month experience or preparation in that place. My only thought during this time was what's next because I have no job, no income, rent to pay, children to feed, and I was in a strange place.

My play mom, Mama Byrd, once told me, "Rene', you and my daughter call yourselves single parents, but you're not. Single parents are out there by themselves with no support from family. Neither of you really know what it means to be a single parent." Suddenly the term, single parent, had a new meaning. Elijah was 6- years-old and upset with the world. I knew it was time for therapy when he raised his voice at me, screaming, "Why did we have to move?" as he knocked everything off my dresser. It was therapy for him, avoiding bail for me. At the same time, Zai'ere was 4- years old and had decided to chew off all of her nails. I was a mommy in distress.

I was able to get unemployment, and God told me to begin working on my plan for my organization, and that's what I did.

In 2010, I became incorporated with the state of North Carolina! Meanwhile, my financial situation was beginning to get worse. My unemployment ran out, and I was denied food stamps, and my car got repossessed. My children and I went weeks sometimes with little to no food, but I tried not to allow them to see or feel the struggle. I cried, mad at God for telling me to move here without a plan to enable me to remain. My sister used to say, "He is the same God, his word stays the same, he got you." I thought and sometimes voiced that it is so much easier to say when you're sitting on the outside looking in. The Holy Spirit used to remind me, *"The earth is the Lord and the fullness therein."* and I would think, so what's the problem? I applied for many jobs and a ton in the school system while praying for one that worked around my babies' school schedules.

While I didn't get any of the jobs I applied for, I received an offer for a job I did not apply for-working as a substitute cafeteria worker, i.e., lunch lady. There was a two-fold blessing behind this job as the schedule was exactly what I had prayed for and needed, and I was able to begin seeing the manifestation of God's direction. In the community where I lived, I saw a need.

Remembering my purpose, I decided to speak with someone at the recreation center about implementing my mentoring program there. How excited I was when the director added ESCAPE (Exiting Social Captivity Applying Power and Education) Mentoring to his program list!!! My mentoring services offered group mentoring twice a week for young ladies ages 12-18 years of age and were free and open to anyone. After ten weeks, we hosted a fashion show that allowed the girls to show off their new look of self-esteem. God's hand and the plan were all up in the mix. Years later, I would come back even better, providing mentoring in the school system, but that's a story for another day. God is not finished with me as my work continues. I am still growing, believing, struggling, and trusting. Because I trust I can keep moving forward.

FROM MAYBE TO YES

Venita James

Finally! The gaps between the hardwood floor planks weren't big enough to ask that they come out to correct them, but big enough to know I would need to get on my knees with a wet rag and a butter knife to clean between them. The last six months were full of frustrating phone calls and barely returned emails, but the result made the process easy to forget. Everything came together beautifully: The quartz countertops and mahogany shelves scattered with cookbooks, colorful dishes arranged to perfection. My cabinet hardware, a blissful blend of vintage and modern, nobody would guess that it took me three trips to the store to find. My kitchen was the embodiment of my most coveted Pinterest boards. But my favorite was the door. In a sea of grey and white, there stood my yellow door. Yellow has never been on my favorite color list. Blue, always. Green at times, but never yellow. Somehow it all worked, and I burst into a huge smile whenever I walked into the room. I was happy here, in this room. Yet as I sat on the floor of my dream kitchen in a small town, Michigan, I was ready to leave it all behind.

When I left my hometown in Charlotte, North Carolina, I had no plans to move back. Although my family and friends were there, I was eager to see what else life had to offer. I never wanted to look back and regret living in Charlotte my entire life. Of course, I would come home to visit. In fact, I wanted to be one of those people who hated traveling on the holidays because the airports are always so crowded. I fantasized about being in the background as the on-site TV news reporter described holiday traffic jams and flight delays. I was ready for a change.

I landed a new job and moved to Minneapolis, Minnesota. I enjoyed exploring a new city and making new friends. I grew to love Minneapolis, May through September. The winter months were a different story. I liked my job for the most part, but as the years passed by, something started to shift. My role no longer excited me. I slowly came to realize it was because my role lacked creativity. I didn't understand how much value I placed on this until it was no longer there. I began to look for another job.

The calls with recruiters were all the same, but one particular call left me curious. A small town I had never heard of in Michigan had a position with a company that was also unfamiliar to me. This was not the move I had in mind. However, this role focused on design and branding. Those were the responsibilities I was passionate about and had prioritized in my job search.

The more I learned about the position and the town I'd move to, the more uncertain I became. I had to choose between living in a small town and loving the work I would do or living in a bigger city and lacking excitement about my day-to-day responsibilities. Confused about whether or not to accept the position, I began to pray. God had guided me so many times before when my path was uncertain. I continued to pray. I prayed some more but was still unclear on an answer. Maybe I wasn't praying the right prayer. Perhaps I wasn't praying hard enough. So I fasted and kept praying, and finally, I heard "maybe." Would God want me to move on a maybe? I decided to accept the offer.

I was excited about my new role and the challenge of reinventing a brand. It was an opportunity to create something that had not yet been. Designing and bringing an idea to life always came naturally. My grandmother taught me to sew at a young age, although I'm sure she regretted it later when I began to cut her dresses for the fabric to sew clothes for my stuffed animals. Even then, I loved the process of bringing an idea to life.

I was happy with my decision to accept this position. I would often hear people say they hate their jobs. I, on the other hand, loved my job. I was one of the lucky few. I was able to research trends, establish brand standards, guide my team on product assortments; this was why I moved. To see little girls twirling in the middle of the grocery store aisle wearing the dresses we created made me beam. Of course, customers didn't know there had been a 2-hour discussion on whether the unicorn on the front should be glitter or sequins. Another winning point was when people like Julie, the cashier at my favorite local bakery, would say our store "actually has cute clothes." Every interaction was validation for a job well done. Our once dilapidated brands were now desirable.

Then came a shift in the atmosphere, very subtle. Barely discernable, not registered on the Richter scale. The success of our brand saw the focus move from design to paperwork and spreadsheets and from creative brainstorming to right-brained processes. There was still so much left to do on the left-brained side to make additional improvements and expand in those areas where we saw success. There were so many ideas left undiscovered, yet instead of building on them, I was redirected to the spreadsheets. Just as the opportunity for creativity drew me to this role, I knew the lack of creativity would not keep me here. I began to feel less like one of the lucky few. At the same time, all the moments that truly mattered, yet I had minimized, slowly became more important. The missed family beach trips and brunches with lifelong friends were events I now longed for. The holiday travel and overcrowded airports were not as glamorous as I had envisioned. My mind began to flood with questions. Was I still happy in my role? What if I up and left?

Should I move back to North Carolina? Again I prayed for answers. "Maybe" was what I heard once more.

My friend and I made a pact when I moved away from Charlotte, that regardless of where we were, we would communicate in some way every day. We kept that pact for years until life got in the way. The challenges of working late into the evening and bath time for the kids made it difficult to exchange more than a few simple pleasantries. On a particular Sunday evening, we finally had a chance to really talk. We were on the phone for hours, but I could tell there was more. Something was left unsaid.

Toward the end of our conversation, my friend finally revealed what she had been holding in. She was pregnant. Her joy was my joy, but that moment held a greater significance. It reminded me of the birth of my nephew that I could not be there for because I lived out of state. I remembered the picture my mother texted me of my grandmother's birthday celebration. I wasn't there because I couldn't find a reasonable flight. She turned 98 that year.

I sank to the kitchen floor as I realized what I had sacrificed. It was at that moment that all the maybes became an overwhelming yes. I didn't completely understand it, but I was determined to stand firm on it and trust God through it. It was there, on my beautiful, hard-to-clean hardwood floors, I decided to quit my job.

Four weeks later, breathing came easier as I walked out the door from my newly former employer and into the parking lot. Now what? People began to ask, "What are you going to do now that you've quit"? My response was always the same, "I'm thinking about starting my own business." It wasn't that I believed it to be true, but because "I don't know" seemed like the wrong answer. I made my way back to North Carolina. I was happy to be home. I had no regrets about my move, no "what ifs" or "I should haves" but lots of "what do I do now that I'm here." I started researching, although I couldn't quite find what I was looking for, probably because I didn't know what I was looking for. I eventually ran out of things to Google.

My dad has always been my biggest cheerleader. He asked that I sit in on a meeting for a project he was leading. It was a development of apartments and retail space, meant to provide housing and accessibility for residents of that community. During the meeting, he began to describe the development, the geometric entryway, the size, and potential use for each building. He was clearly excited, but it was evident by the furrowed brows of the others in the room that they were struggling to see his vision. It was clear to me that he needed a brand tool, a brochure, perhaps, to help others understand what had not yet come to fruition. I knew I could help. My dad used that brochure more like a bragging tool and less as the communication tool for which it was intended. Regardless, people started to take note. One person asked if I had a business card, another asked if I had a website. I lied and said yes to both. Now, reader, lying is not a regular habit of mine. But this felt less like a lie and more like a not yet. I also knew that I now had to make good on it. That little white lie became my motivation to bring it to fruition. It also meant that I had to think beyond a brochure. I had to create a way for people to reach me. I needed a name, a logo, a brand. Is this truly a business? *Maybe.*

I could say that one little brochure launched Mali Creative, a design, and creative consulting company, but that wouldn't be the whole story. Consider the seasons of uncertainty, the sleepless nights, and the realization that my time living and learning outside of North Carolina served a greater purpose. I gained an irrational peace when I walked away from a highly paid position. While I was completely unsure of the path, I trusted God to lead the way. Consider how people and projects continued to reveal themselves in a way that could have only been positioned by God. Yes, putting my gifts on display in that little brochure gave me a needed boost, but Mali Creative was launched by trusting God through all the subtle shifts in energy and when a series of maybes turned into one big yes.

DARE TO DREAM AGAIN

Juanita Corry Jackson

My story is about finding the courage to walk the path that leads to realizing my dream. Let me say right off the top, maintaining that walk was not easy. Moving from vision to reality took work, faith, prayer, determination, and a few coaches along the way. One of my mentors, Mr. Les Brown, said, "You have greatness inside of you." The truth is we all have greatness within us. However, we may need help in recognizing our greatness due to fears and insecurities. Our awesomeness is often throbbing under life-inflicted wounds or buried treasure concealed in a chest of pain and worry.

Let me say my story did not start with me being the established entrepreneur I am today. My phenomenal grandparents raised me and provided a humble yet excellent beginning. Neither my mother nor my father was available during those early years of my life. When it comes to molding and shaping my mind into the woman I am today; the award goes to my grandparents and a little to the school of hard knocks.

I remember growing up, dreaming, and believing that one day I would own my own business and make a lot of money that would enable me to give back to my family and others. I saw myself speaking in churches and on stages, riding in a limo, and having a staff. That day would come. However, I also had another dream. I am not sure if it was my dream or someone else's dream for me. That was the dream of becoming a wife and mother, having a good job with a beautiful home and two cars. This was a true "Leave It to Beaver" style dream. Any chance of starting out in a traditional "Leave it to Beaver" scenario ended when I became a mom at the age of eighteen years old. The dream seemed even further from my grasp when I had my second child at twenty-two. There was no husband in sight, and I figured that dream was dead. There is a verse in the Bible that I love, which says, *"In the last days, I will send my Spirit on all men. Then your sons and daughters will speak God's Word. Your old men will dream dreams. Your young men will see special dreams"*. - *Joel 2:28 (NLT)*.

In its most simple terms, this means that God has a way in which He shows us a glimpse of what's possible.

Despite having two children and feeling as if marriage wasn't in the cards for me, in 1986 at age twenty-three, just a year after my second child was born, I got married. This dream had nothing to do with owning my business or speaking on stages. This was the "Leave it to Beaver Dream". I was on my way to having the beautiful home and the perfect life.

Within my first year of marriage came baby number three, and for twenty-three of the twenty-five years of marriage, I was living my dream. Through my husband's infidelity and a child born from the affair of which my husband was the father, I remained 100% invested. Then the unexpected happened, I prayed to God for a change. The word that I kept hearing over and over was surrender. A couple of days later, I had my dream again! My business! I had earned my real estate license in 2009 but kept working a full-time job because we needed the income. I had a family, a mortgage, a car payment, and private school tuition for my youngest two.

In 2010 I was diagnosed with a brain tumor. I had enough faith to believe God for complete healing of the tumor. I was not going to have my head shaved, and I was not having brain surgery. God was going to complete His Word in me. I can happily say he did just that!! I thought how my faith was so strong with God and my healing, but I did not have the faith for my business, life, or my true passion. Again in a whisper, the word surrender continued to repeat in my spirit. At the end of 2010 I decided to heed God's word. I surrendered to the spirit to follow my real estate career and see where it would take me. Needless to say, as with most new businesses, the money did not rush in. In fact, the money ran out, and so did my husband. Truth be told, he hadn't been invested in our family for a long time. When my marriage ended, I believe all this came to teach me that I am worth so much more.

The divorce was my last and final payment to a 25-year marriage, which became one of the best investments I made in myself! Along the way, I told myself that I stayed as long as I did for the kids. As grown adults, they told me they wished we would have divorced sooner. They like today's version of me now a whole lot better. I had a dream, I fulfilled the dream, and I lived to dream again. Don't think that just because you went down one path that it's too late to try another route if you feel led to do so. Just dust the cobwebs off your dreams and dream again. If you can dream it and believe it, it's possible to receive it! Would you believe me if I told you that the dream is just the first glimpse of what could be? The dream is your vision. However, once seen, the dream then needs to be written down. We need to bring it to life. Writing gives our dreams, meaning, and purpose.

One of the things that I have learned from contract law in the real estate business is to elevate our verbal agreement to writing. Although my words have power in and of themselves, the written word becomes permanent. A written contract can't be changed without approval from all parties involved. This is how you need to think about your dreams and your promises to yourself. I often think now about my words having creative power. We are creative beings.

There is a story in the Bible of Jesus, who was tempted by the devil. This temptation came after He had fasted 40 days and 40 nights. The devil mocked Jesus, saying if you are who you say you are, do this. If you do this, I will give you that. What is essential in the story is Jesus' reply. He combats the enemy by saying, "It is written." There is POWER in making a statement. Often the enemy is not the devil, as we know from the biblical stories. Sometimes the devil manifests as well-intended people who try to crush your dreams. Occasionally, we have to take the bold step to write down, to breathe life into our dreams.

The written word serves as a road map of a planned destination. As you read the vision, you can now apply turn by turn directions of how you plan to get to your destination. The turns are goals, or small steps necessary to prepare for the journey you are about to undertake. Remember, there will be detours and roadblocks along the way, but always remember your rallying cry, "It is written."

I would encourage all my faithpreneurs to know that whatever you set your mind and heart to is possible. Be intentional, deliberate, and learn to surrender. Realize it is okay not to know everything and to rely on someone else who might have the answer you need. Give credit along the way to all those who help you reach your next level. When I was able to give up the "Leave it to Beaver" dream and walk into my purpose, life became fun to live and gave me the ability to strive for more. I spent twenty-five years in a marriage trying to be something I was not designed to be past that season. Yet I am thankful for all the lessons and victories that came as a result.

Today, I am now Pastor and Overseer of several churches. I speak and train not just in my churches but in other churches.

Speaking and training is a big part of my purpose, of what I believe I was sent to the earth to do. I didn't always know that, but today it is written in my life. I also own a real estate company, where I not only have the privilege of selling traditional real estate, I also have several investor clients that I currently train and mentor in how to invest in real estate. I am a business partner in a financial literacy company, helping to implement and create secure financial futures for its customers. I am also an Author, Speaker, Trainer, and Coach certified through the great Mr. Les Brown. I have just touched the surface of all the possibilities available for my life.

I have greatness inside of me, and so do you. I have come to learn that no matter what happens, if there is a tomorrow, there is an opportunity for better. We are privileged to have experienced everything we've been through: the good, the ugly, and everything in between. We can take a leap of faith to the unknown, or we can stay right where we are.

No matter where you are on the spectrum, whether it's from humble beginnings, or "splendaciously" wealthy, stuck is stuck, so never lose sight of your dreams. Never stop believing you can accomplish anything through faith and God's word. In all the things, we have to keep moving forward. There is a short bible verse that guides me. It has helped me through many a challenge. I'm sharing it with you with the hope that it will strengthen you as well:

"I can do all things because Christ gives me the strength." -
Philippians 4:13 (NLT)

Dream it. Write it down. Do it. Dream Again. You will be ready for your turn by turn steps, prepared to walk the path to your purpose.

PAIN TO PROSPERITY

Moreale P Brown

I was born during the cold, festive month of December in 1963 in beautiful, historic Charleston, South Carolina. Charleston is also called the Holy City. I was the seventh of ten children. Before I was born, I had a brother to die at childbirth, and a sister passed at seven years old. My dedicated mother is Albertha Gaillard, and my father is James Brown, no not the singer and entertainer. During the sixties, there weren't a lot of social service programs to provide aid for children in Charleston. Consequently, my strong and persuasive grand-mom, Anna Brown, told my mother to relocate to the Big Apple. So around 1966, mom moved to Brooklyn, New York, the home of the Brooklyn Dodgers.

My mother and father weren't married. I recall my father coming by to pick me up to take me to buy shoes. Around the age of 7, he stopped coming by to visit. When I got older, I asked my mother why he stopped his visits. She said it was because she wouldn't have sex with him. I asked myself, "How could a man desert his child? In the midst of my life struggles, one of my major pain points was the abandonment of my father.

I am complete, yet there are some valuable things a father is wired to provide that I never received.

My father gave me 23 chromosomes, and I am alive. It hurts that I do not remember what he looks like. I don't recall his voice or his scent. At age 56, I still get teary-eyed writing about one of the most important individuals in the world, my dad. According to Focus on the Family, involved **fathers** – especially biological **fathers** – bring positive benefits to their children that no other person is as likely to bring. They provide protection and economic support and male role models.

According to *Orphan Statistics from Children on the Brink 2004;* 24 million children in the U.S. live apart from their biological fathers. Because of these staggering numbers, many children, youth, and families fall prey to the following:

- Malnutrition, poverty, illiteracy
- Radical belief systems, human trafficking, sexual exploitation, illicit sexual behaviors
- Drugs, gangs, AIDS
· Hopelessness

Yes, fatherlessness is an epidemic, yet God equipped me to overcome those challenges. I authored a book about my experiences called the "Unending Love of a Father."

My mother desired to live in a habitable apartment, but with seven children, landlords were reluctant to rent to her. My older sister, Evon, was raised by my grandmother, Anna Brown. I remember one of the apartments was deemed suitable by my mother. We rented it, but the apartment was freezing on a near arctic level. Most mornings, my mother heated water on the stove so that all seven of her children could wash up and get ready for school. Even though we were living in these conditions, I knew early on that I had a greater purpose in life. I just did not know what my purpose was. I know that I beat out millions of sperms cells to have a spiritual experience in the natural earth. I believe that I was born to be an entrepreneur.

Mom wanted her own home to have a permanent place for all of us. But she was always struggling to make ends meet. As a child, I rejoiced on the 13th and the 28th of each month. Those were the dates that my mother's welfare check came in the mail; we called it "Check Day." Government Assistance was like a biweekly Christmas to me. I recall mom pacing the floors and crying out to God for help. She constantly gave us pep talks about the importance of education and a strong work ethic. She would say to the girls, "Keep your skirt down and hit the books." I am not sure how my mother raised eight children and stayed sane.

One sunny day my siblings and I came home from school, she gave us the good news about moving to a section of newly built Public Housing in the East New section of Brooklyn. Moving from the cold apartment felt like we were moving into a brand-new home. We felt just like the characters from The

Jefferson's TV Show. We began to sing the lyrics, "Well we're moving on up! To the east side. To a de-luxe apartment in the sky-yy."

It was called the Model City Public Housing Authority. I have some great memories growing up in Public Housing. Our neighbors' parents watched out for us as we played handball, skelly, punch ball, kickball, and chased boys. The downside was when my neighbor told my mother that I was kissing a boy in the backyard. Yes, I went through a "boy-crazy" phase.

Although God provided for us, I knew that there was a realm of abundance that God wanted my mother and her family to tap into. My sixth-grade teacher, Mrs. Manpou, inspired me to grow and learn. I recall writing an essay entitled, "If I was a millionaire, three things that I would do. "My three things were easy. First, I would buy my mother a house for $250,000. Then I would give my mother $250,000. I'd give $250,000 to the poor and keep the remaining $250,000 for myself. I've always had a generous heart to help the poor and broken-hearted. My decision to be an entrepreneur is birthed out of pain, passion, and purpose. However, it is faith and the desire to lead that keeps me pushing forward to my great destiny. I am a leader in God's eternal Kingdom, and I help others to lead.

As a Kingdom Builder and world changer, I need faith, favor, and finance to change the trajectory of family, education, economics, leadership, and government. What is faith? Faith defined is complete trust or confidence in someone or something. It's also a strong belief in God or a religious doctrine based on spiritual substance hoped for or not seen. For me, faith is like having a sixth sense or determination about the future. I knew that I did not want to live in poverty for the rest of my life. As I watched my mother trust God in the difficult times, I began to use daring faith to overcome the hurdles of abandonment and move towards upward mobility.

Before I graduated with my Associate's Degree, I had an insight that I was going to graduate with a Master's Degree, and I told my friends about my plans. They couldn't understand why I'd even think about achieving a Master's when I didn't yet have my Associates. Stating my plans helped solidify my goals. I did, as I said, earning my Masters' degree in General Education and Special Education. I was the first in my family to go to college.

I experienced an extremely traumatizing season in the eighties when I was in my twenties. My three older brothers did not make healthy lifestyle choices, which resulted in their untimely deaths. Sid died in 1986 from drug misuse. Then one year later, my oldest brother, Byron, who was like a father to me, died. My brother Wendell died in 1998. My mother lost a total of 5 children. Around this same time, my best friend Vicky got strung out on drugs.

Things were changing in our deluxe apartment complex. East New York became a war zone. Due to drug wars, young thugs who attended the same church as my mother participated in shoot outs around 3 p.m. almost daily. One sunny day, just as my young friends and I were leaving Phyllis Wheatley Elementary, a gunfight broke out on my block. I knew both perpetrators, and they were neighbors. Nevertheless, they were attempting to kill each other. Theft increased as well. One of my neighbors broke into an apartment directly next to ours. This was so stressful! I fully empathize with children who live in unsafe neighborhoods.

During this point in my life, I knew that a good income would be a catalyst for living in a better neighborhood. Then my mother and I were the only ones left in the apartment due to the marriages of my other siblings. Eventually, we moved to Rockaway Parkway, which was a much better community. Drugs came our way there also. As a result, we experienced the same negative consequences from before. I lived there for 12 years, making a total of 33 years of project living. That was 33 years too long!

I had a burning desire to purchase a house, so I worked three different positions at the Board of Education but still could not afford to buy a home in Brooklyn, New York. As a result, in 2005, I finally saved up enough money to buy a Condominium in New Jersey. So, I relocated from the multicultural, electric, and fast-paced New York City to the beautiful, slower-paced suburbs of Maplewood New Jersey.

In 2007, there was a massive layoff from the Newark Board of Education, which included me. I had purchased my Condominium in 2005. I was paying $1,400 in mortgage and approximately $300.00 for the Associations maintenance. I was only able to keep my mortgage going for one year after the layoff. In 2008, I realized that I did not have any more savings to pay my mortgage and maintenance. I became stressed to the max. I was looking for a breakthrough, but God wanted me to be free of all the debt. He knew that a loan modification would not wipe out the debt. According to the nonprofit National Bureau of Economic Research, Wikipedia, the U.S. recession began in December 2007 and ended in June 2009. Personally, the recession I experienced lasted from 2008 to 2017.

In 2010, the Holy Spirit directed me to go onto the Newark Preschool website. I went on the website and saw the job posting for a Family Worker Coordinator. Wow! I was super excited to apply for this job. I eagerly revised my resume and filled out the job application. I had a two day turn around to get the application in before the deadline, but I got it all in on time.

This was literally my "dream job." I worked in the Social Work Department at the Headquarters office. As Family Worker Coordinator, I had the awesome responsibility of coaching, supporting, supervising, and training a staff of 20 Family Workers. I provided 17-20 trainings per year to my staff and engaged in agency-wide trainings. During my tenure at

NPC, I received the Train-The-Trainer certificate. My fellow coordinator and I streamlined the enrollment intake process and created a best practice handbook for parents, which was adopted by the Family Outreach Program, Prevent Child Abuse New Jersey. But in 2014, NPC's contract wasn't renewed.

After the layoff, I felt that my tenure in New Jersey was over. This lay off was different, it blasted me out of New Jersey, and I landed in North Carolina. My brother, Pastor Johnny E. Brown, moved to Charlotte, North Carolina, over 30 years ago. He wanted a better life for him and his family. His prayer was for his siblings to move to Charlotte with him. So, I prayed about relocating to Charlotte and got the release to move in 2014. In 2016, I lost the Condominium due to foreclosure, but God miraculously allowed the Mortgage Company and Creditors to cancel all my debt. This trial lasted for 10 years. Spiritually, the number 10 symbolizes completeness.

I had experienced three layoffs in my lifetime, and each one set me back financially. In 2019 I am declaring, "No More Lay Offs." I am tired of giving 100% only to be downsized. That's one of the reasons why I have chosen to use my gifts toward entrepreneurship. I look at circumstances and focus on who God is. As you can see, enterprise requires faith. During seasons of adversity, it is my faith in the living God which keeps me persevering as an entrepreneur. For additional income, I continue to work as a Substitute Teacher from 6:45 a.m. to 2:15

p.m. As a Substitute Teacher, I have the pleasure of serving approximately 90-120 students daily, ranging from 14-17 years old. Teaching is my primary gift, so as a Certified Teacher, I give 100% to teach, train, and equip our dynamic students to prepare them for the 21st Century. I think it's vital as an entrepreneur to be flexible with your income-producing activities. You may have to seek part-time employment to allow you to keep your entrepreneurial dreams afloat.

I work two part-time jobs and my business, and sometimes I work so hard that I do not realize how much time and energy I am investing to make ends meet. Despite all of my hard work, sometimes I am still in the land of "not enough or just enough." I know my season is coming. I am blessed because I consistently substitute, sharing my craft daily. I also work as a part-time Health Care Assistant (HCA), where I work 8-24 hours per month. There I stand in the gap for seniors and medically fragile clients who are battling Alzheimer's/Dementia.

I will persevere to see what God will do through me as His kingdom builder. He has empowered me to remember him, for it is he that giveth thee the power to get wealth, that he may establish his covenant which he swore unto thy fathers, as it is this day. - Deuteronomy 8:18.

The name of my business is Moreale Brown Inc. We are a Consulting and Training business. Our motto is: Optimize your Abilities to Achieve Maximum Impact. My business was registered in 2016, and I have been working on the foundation and back office. My largest clients are Livingstone College and Inspired Life Church.

THE LILIES OF THE FIELD

Perkine D. Theus

So why do you worry about clothing? Consider the lilies of the field, how they grow: they neither toil nor spin; and yet I say to you that even Solomon in all his glory was not arrayed like one of these. Now if God so clothes the grass of the field, which today is, and tomorrow is thrown into the oven, will He not much more clothe you, O you of little faith? - Matthew 6:28 -30 (NKJV)

When I look at my twelve-year-old daughter, full of joy and grace, a beautiful young girl with a bright future ahead of her, I imagine myself at her age. I loved to sing and dance, and I especially loved art. As I am looking at her, she calls out, "Mom!"

I awoke from my daydream. My daughter looked at me and said, "Mom, it is time to share your story!" I thought about what she said. Yes, my story! So that a young girl within a woman can be set free or a young boy within a man can be set free. I paused as I stood in the room, looking around for some type of confirmation. My mentor was there, and I shared what my daughter told me. Her response was, "From the mouth of a babe." They encouraged me to write so I could be free from what held me in bondage.

When I was a child, I was not afraid to take chances. No fear to ask a homeless man to help me cross an intersection. I recalled that man telling me he was a veteran of Vietnam. I always had the desire one day to provide shelter for the veterans. During the course of my life, that desire was altered. In the summer of 1989, I was twelve years old, full of energy, and I loved to dress up. I was a young girl, lively and vibrant like a light. But something caused the brightness to turn dim, darkening. My parents were not home; they had to run errands. I was growing, developing, and needed to take a nap. As I was sleeping, I felt a hand slip into my undies, and those fingers went into my secret place. I was numb and could not move because I was in a state of shock. A teenage male violated me. He informed me that if I were to share what happened with anyone, including my parents, I would not be taken seriously. He said everyone would think I was crazy, and I'd be placed in a mental hospital.

That teenager turned my life upside down. I felt worthless and disgraced. I battled with low self-esteem, and I had lost the desire to be the stylish girl I once loved. I could not hear compliments that I was pretty because I thought that I was ugly. I spent part of my life blaming myself for what transpired. My family began to notice a difference in me. I was withdrawn, and I did not care so much about my appearance. They thought that I was just going through the phase of pre-adolescence. However, I was still afraid to share my trauma with them. I spent the remainder of my early age being ashamed of who I was, searching for answers.

As the years passed, I began to develop shortness of breath and depression. I had thoughts of taking my life. There were times when I would picture my funeral and who would be there. There were times I had anxiety attacks where I felt like I was choking. Then finally, my mom decided to take me to the doctor. My doctor gathered all the symptoms that I was complaining about and prescribed anti-depressants and referred me to an adolescent counselor. My healing has been a process and still is a process that I deal with every day. I struggled in school, and I wanted to quit. There were times I heard voices within that said I was worthless. I would look in the mirror and think I was a disgrace.

My father would have alcohol for casual drinking when his friends came over. At the age of fourteen, when no one was around, I drank to numb the pain that I felt. Meanwhile, I started hanging around with "project kids." I remember my junior high earth science teacher encouraged me to stop hanging in the projects. I never listened until the day I saw someone get shot in front of me. I changed course and continued to go to counseling.

The trauma of my assault stayed with me. I did not share what had happened to me with my therapist during my sessions. It was not until I saw the news about the priests who molested boys in the Catholic churches that I was able to talk to anyone about my sexual assault. I could relate to those boys. Seeing the news allowed me to process my situation, and when I look back, I knew it was God's timing, and it was ok for me to open up.

I recalled when I was a freshman in high school. My English teacher assigned the book by Maya Angelou, *I Know Why the Caged Bird Sings*. As I read the novel, a chapter spoke about Maya being sexually assaulted as a preteen by her mother's boyfriend. It was as if I was reading about my incident. The outcome was that her trial became her triumph. Her story also inspired me and set me on the path to my healing.

Meanwhile, My God sent signs of wonder to me. These signs let me know that I was special in His sight even though I did not feel his immediate presence. Once when I went to counseling, I noticed a picture on the wall of footprints in the sand on a beach. It was a reminder that God's presence was with me. One day on BET, I watched a performance of the song "Optimistic" by the Sounds of Blackness. The song was so encouraging. I remember going to the music store and buying the CD. I would listen to the lyrics that said, *"You can win, as long as you keep your head to the sky!"* That song followed me on the path to healing and restoration. Each time I would hear the song, it was like a lion roaring inside of me. I knew that I could make it.

During my years in high school, I found teachers that became my mentors. They would encourage and speak life into me. I did not share with them or my parents what happened to me. I'm not sure why. Maybe the words from that teenage molester had punctured my soul more than I realized. Would they believe me? Would they think I was crazy? Besides, what was the point after all these years?

My parents always prayed for me, and they loved me. My mother would watch Joyce Myers sermons on television, and one day Joyce Myers shared with the audience about her sexual abuse by her father. I began to feel more and more that I was not the only one. I felt a sense of peace. Why bring up that horrible period of my life? I had moved on, or so I thought.

After high school, I decided to go to college and major in psychology. During my first semester, if there was a party, I was there drinking and having a great time with my peers. My grades suffered. I had to get my act together. I was blessed to have a fantastic learning specialist who was on my case and wanted me to succeed. The next semester I made it to the Dean's list.

As I neared graduation, I needed to complete an internship. God blessed me with a position as a Rehab Specialist with two ladies who suffered from traumatic brain injury (TBI). Their experience was my wake up call to change my lifestyle of partying and drinking. I was still going to counseling, but I needed something to fill the void from partying. Soul searching to complete the emptiness, I filled that void with food. The food didn't do it. I tried everything, even attending a Buddhist temple as a Christian, but I still felt empty. One day, The Lord revealed His mercy and His love to me.

That day started pretty regularly. I was working with my TBI clients, and it was time for me to administer their medications. I had accidentally locked the keys inside the office where their medicines were stored. One of the women was very upset about having to take her pills late. I recalled she went to her room and fell asleep. I was so worried, I stood in front of the door and said, "Jesus, you said to speak and the mountain moves. Show me your power! Please open the door." The door popped open. I stood frozen, and I was able to give my client her medication. From there, I knew the Lord was with me. No matter what I faced, he never left me. I continued working as a Rehab Specialist.

It was during this time that my co-worker introduced me to real estate and real estate investing. She explained briefly about rental properties. I was young, still in college, majoring in Psychology, and did not take her seriously. Looking back, I regret not paying better attention. Meanwhile, my mentor invited me to a network marketing meeting on a gift incentive. I thought about how I could introduce this product into the workplace. I shared the concept with a friend, and they referred me to an organization that helps women to become entrepreneurs.

I met with a business consultant from the organization, and we developed a relationship where she became like my sister from another mother. I shared with her my interest in using the gift incentive in the workplace, incorporating my TBI experience, and what I learned as a psychology major. She asked if I had thought about coaching. I did not know what coaching was. She then explained to me coaching was inspiring someone to reach their potential within. Then I thought about my work and realized that I had been coaching my TBI clients by giving them constant encouragement and teaching them the skills they needed to succeed.

I started going to seminars and workshops. Then at the age of 23, I decided I wanted to become a life coach in the workplace. One seminar I attended had a well-known author and life coach guest speaker at the event. I had the chance to speak to her. I explained to her that I was planning to become a Life Coach. She asked if I had life experience. I told her that I had just graduated from college and was working as a Rehab Specialist. She responded, "First get the life experience and then become a life coach." I was not happy with her response. How did she know what kind of life journey I'd had?

Eventually, I graduated from college with a BS degree and got married. After working as a Rehab Specialist for five years, I decided to try corporate America, and I realized that the environment was not for me. So I signed up to work with a staffing agency and was sent to various places. I had the chance to meet with people, and they would share their life stories with me. I would give them a word of hope.

A year into my marriage, my husband and I decided to take a road trip to Hinesville, GA. My cousin and a close family friend were in the military at Fort Stewart. I thought about the veteran who helped me crossed the street and my co-worker who introduced me to the idea of buying rental properties. I talked with my husband about purchasing a rental property that would attract active military members and their families. My husband was on board. Our friend referred us to a real estate agent. We found a house, and as we were in the process of buying it as a rental property, I began to think about the difficulties of renting out of state. I allowed fear to take over, and we backed off. I regret what I did, but God had a greater plan for me.

My dear friend, the business consultant, and her family had moved to North Carolina. She encouraged my husband and me to come to visit. We went to Mint Hill, where she and her family reside. My husband and I fell in love with the state. We purchased our first home just outside of Charlotte. We went back to Massachusetts, packed our belongings, moved, and started a family in our new surroundings. I still had not shared with my parents my darkest secret.

My husband and I had two daughters. I became a stay-at-home mom and cared for my children and my home. I would play Christian and gospel music in the house to take away my fear and anxiety about the thought of not being a fit mother. I would sing and dance. My children thought I was a joyful mom and that I loved to bake and cook. As my girls became toddlers, I decided to go back into the mental health field and work on the weekend part-time.

One day I decided to share my story with my best friend, and she suggested that I share it with my mother. When my mother came to visit, I was finally able to tell her what had happened to me. She was distraught and sad because I waited so long to tell her. I tried to explain to her why. She was hurt, and I understood because I was now a mother. We were both able to come to an understanding as to why it took as long as it did. There was so much relief because it was no longer a secret from my mother

I worked as a Behavioral Specialist with adults on the weekend. I helped individuals who were traumatized by life events. I came across young women and men who were sexually assaulted. Hearing their stories, I realized how fortunate I was not to have ended up in a mental hospital. Over the years, I worked as a coach, guiding the people I served to reach their potential. One of the residents doubted himself about getting a job. I encouraged him to speak as though he had the job. He was hired and has been there since.

The work I was doing for my clients reminded me of the benefits of counseling, so I decided to return to therapy. My counselor had suggested I read, "The Healing Soul of a

Woman," by Joyce Meyers. The author helped me to have a different perspective of myself, knowing that God will take my pain and turn it around for my good. After reading the book, I decided to join an Adult Survivor of Child Abuse group. As I continued to attend the group, the host offered me a position as a co-host. Eventually, she had to leave the group for personal reasons, and I became the host of the group. Being a host was a significant part of my healing. I continued my work as a Behavioral Specialist, as well.

Now I have clarity of what life coaching means and why I needed life experience. My plan is to one day open a place of refuge for veterans.

The End

MEET THE AUTHORS

TAMI L STEWART

Tami L. Stewart was born and raised in Washington, DC. She left the DC area to attend Belmont Abbey College in Belmont, North Carolina. After graduation, Tami moved to Charlotte, North Carolina where she resides today. She is married and has one son.

Tami has a love for the Arts and all things creative. Her interest in jewelry started at an early age. Over the years she developed a passion for making jewelry that resulted in the creation of her handmade jewelry business, Totally Tamz. Her slogan is "The Look for Less" Original designs at affordable prices.

Today you will find Tami sharing her gifts and talents with others interested in learning the basics of jewelry making. Her hope is that someone else will be inspired to start the journey down their pathway to entrepreneurship. She moves at the pace of grace as she takes a daily walk in obedience.

Tami can be reached at
www.etsy.com/shop/totallytamz/
IG @TotallyTamz

RENÈE CHOLMONDELEY

Renee Cholmondeley currently resides in Charlotte, N.C. by way of New York City, and Long Island. I am first and foremost a child of the living God. At a very close second, the mother of adult twins who are amazing people that I am very proud to know and honored that He chose me to carry their lives for a short time. I take comfort in thinking that I'm a good, loyal friend to some the most amazing women that I've ever met on this planet; you know who you are. I have a uniquely blended family, some of us by blood, but most of us by Spirit where I'm the Big Sister. I like to think I'm having an impact on those that I serve with in my ministry. My life is my work.

Renèe can be reached at
renee.cholmondeley@gmail.com

EBONEE BRYANT-LINDSAY

Ebonee Bryant-Lindsay made her entrance into the world during the 'Blizzard of 1983' in Brooklyn, New York on February 13, 1983. She was born in the Big Apple, but was raised in the small town of Inkster, Michigan outside of the Motor City. Ebonee lives in the Queen City of Charlotte North Carolina with her husband and two wonderful boys. She has been in Sales and Service much of her career and is currently building her own arts and crafts business. You might find Ebonee wandering the aisles of her happy place, Hobby Lobby, always with the next craft project in mind. During her years as a stay-at-home mom she wrote poems and songs, and created homemade gifts and wedding decor. She also enjoys upcycling furniture, painting, and interior design.

You can reach her at
ebonee.bryantlindsay@gmail.com
980-522-8850.

TAMRA TOLBERT-BUSH

Tamra Tolbert-Bush is a loving wife, and a mother of 4 with a genuine heart. Her passion for people drives her to educate, uplift, and nurture her clients toward financial improvement. She is knowledgeable in the areas of real estate investing, asset protection, and finance with decades of experience. She is a licensed insurance agent, with a bachelor's degree in Project management from AIU, and a certification in paralegal studies from Canisius College. Growing up in the Langfield projects of Buffalo, NY has taught her that the lack of information, and proper planning can limit access to resources, and diminish a person's hope for their future. Because of this, Tamra eventually decided to start a consulting business offering a range of services that helps people make healthy financial decisions.

Tamra can be reached @ 704-449-9962

https://www.facebook.com/mstamtol

www.instragram.com/iam_tamra_official

Ph. No. 980-522-8498

E. info@source1associates.com

www.source1associates.com

www.facebook.com/source1associates

www.instagram.com/source1associates_official

YouTube: Source1associates

BELINDA SPEARS

Belinda Spears thought about becoming a missionary, like Mother Theresa. A burning desire gripped Belinda, to help others recover from being sick. Destined to answer the call, Belinda became a nurse and served for thirty plus years.

As a young, faith entrepreneur, Belinda experienced business opportunities that were short-lived. Yet, Belinda's main goal is to inspire and empower people to go through life challenges by exposing them to the Word of Truth in Christian short stories.

On a rainy day, the Lord imprinted within Belinda's heart that He was her Shepherd. Listen, He is your Shepherd, too. Regardless of life's hardships, He will carry you through, step by step. Just keep the faith, and watch the Lord do the impossible!

You can contact Belinda at
spearsbelinda425@gmail.com

CASEY CHINEDU IFEDI

Casey Chinedu Ifedi is a licensed Realtor and Property Manager in the state of North Carolina. From student housing, real estate consultation and real estate investing; both professionally and personally, Mr. Ifedi works with clients to create a practical and holistic real estate strategy. Mr. Ifedi brings a team of lenders, credit experts, and qualified professionals that work together to bring the client the highest quality in service and representation.

As a graduate and former student-housing advisor at East Carolina University, Mr. Ifedi worked to improve the student housing experience. While a student at ECU, Casey was able to create The T.E.A.M., which created open dialogue between students and faculty in improving and enhancing the on-campus experience. Through this opportunity Casey has been able to transition his time on campus to a full time real estate career focused on maximizing the management, profit margins, and overall well-being of every client.

Email: Casey_3010@yahoo.com
Number:704-301-8399
IG: C.Ifedi   Facebook: GenChinedu

STEPHANIE D MORRIS

Meet Stephanie D. Morris--The Connector & Wealth Building Maven!

"Life is meaningless if you are not connected to the desires of your heart and living a passionate life of purpose!"

Stephanie's lifelong goal is to build generational wealth through real estate and business ownership. As a multi-passionate entrepreneur, Stephanie has several businesses that will touch many facets of a person's need. Through L&S Cutting Edge Properties LLC, she buys homes and rents them to families. SDM Epic Travel offers a way for people to travel the world. SDM Connections Enterprises LLC allows her to coach others in discovering their passions and purpose through vision board workshops and her new journal *"31 Days to the Heart of My Purpose"*.

To connect with Stephanie
smorris368@gmail.com
Twitter: @sdmconnections

RENE' BREWER

Rene' T. Brewer is a mental health strategist and a single mother of three teens. A native of Chicago, she has resided in Charlotte, NC since 2008. Currently she is an instructor at Central Piedmont Community College. Rene' recently received her Masters of Science in Clinical Mental Health Counseling from Capella University. She is a member of Chi Sigma Iota Honor Society and American Counseling Association. Her proudest moment is the establishment of ESCAPE, an organization that promotes mental health awareness and mentoring. As the Founder of ESCAPE, Rene' is responsible for providing mentoring for youth and promoting mental health awareness within schools, organizations and agencies. Her organization promotes and supports the collaboration between parents, students and community partners to assist in making changes that help individuals go beyond where others set limits.

Feel free to contact Rene'
mhstrategist@yahoo.com
or phone 704-247-7456.

VENITA JAMES

Venita James is a Charlotte native. She studied at Savannah College of Art & Design.

She began her career at Belk using color and design to create seasonal trends for multiple apparel brands. Her journey continued at Target, where she focused on brand development and aligning design needs with the right partners to commercialize apparel from idea to launch.

Venita was then presented with an opportunity to lead the product development team at Meijer, a midwest apparel and grocery retailer. As Director, she led the relaunch of their proprietary sportswear and activewear brands. By clearly establishing brand standards and through strategic use of color and design, formerly traditional brands became relevant.

Having relocated back to Charlotte, Venita has launched Mali Creative; a design services and consulting company. She believes every brand has a voice. The goal of Mali Creative is to amplify it to show people what's possible.

To contact Venita
Instagram & Facebook @Mali.Creative

JUANITA CORRY JACKSON

Juanita Corry Jackson, an Author and CEO of Creative Global Management Solutions, Inc. She is the Overseer of I Believe God Ministries International, Inc and Pastor of I Believe God Ministries Charlotte. She is a Speaker, Trainer and Coach that received her certification through the Les Brown Maximum Achievement Team.

website: www.juanitacorrryjackson.com

Email: info@juanitacorryjackson.com

phone: 980-292-0975

https://m.facebook.com/juanitacorryjackson/?ref=page_inter nal&mt_nav=0

Instagram.com@juanitacorry

twitter.twitter.com/JuanitaJrealty

inkedIn.com/JuanitaJuanitaCorryJackson

https://authorcentral.amazon.com/gp/profile

MOREALE P BROWN

Moreale P. Brown is an author, speaker and business owner. She is the CEO of Moreale Brown Inc., a company that helps individuals and organizations Achieve Maximum Impact.

As a Leadership and Life Coach, she has worked with several organizations such as Newark Preschool Council, Inc., Inspired Life Church and Living Stone College to name a few.

Moreale is a Certified Teacher at CMS and Facilitator at Elevation Leadership Pipeline Class.

Brown holds a Master's degree in Childhood Education/Special Education. Also, Project Management certificate from Central Piedmont Community College.

Brown is a "Train the Trainer" through (AEYC). Member of Sarasota School of Christian Counseling.

Moreale was featured on Empowerment Publishing & Multi-Media. Co-created a parent handbook recognized by the NJ Prevent Child Abuse Family Outreach program.

Moreale P. Brown lives in North Carolina and loves to go to the Billiard.

For bookings call 704-621-4860 or www.morealebrowninc.com.

PERKINE D THEUS

Perkine D. Theus is an inspirational speaker who is passionate about encouraging individuals to find their purpose in life. She holds a Bachelor of Science Degree in Bereavement Studies.

As an overcomer of childhood abuse, she works as a Behavioral Specialist and hosts a group for Anonymous Survivors of adult child abuse. Her favorite phase is, "Where there is a will, there is away."

Perkine is a proud wife and mother of two precious girls. She loves spending time with her family and likes to travel. In her quiet time, she enjoys meditating on scriptures from the Bible.

Contact Perkine at
pdenoyes@gmail.com

Made in the USA
Monee, IL
20 January 2020

20568380R00085